"This is a desperately needed and helpful book. I devoured it in one sitting. I couldn't put it down."

Rick Warren, founding pastor
Saddleback Church

"Chad Brand has helped to fill a lacuna on the subject of work, economics, and civic stewardship in the Baptist tradition. Serving as something of a primer, *Flourishing Faith* examines key issues related to political economy such as vocational calling, wealth, government, and taxation. Interesting, informative, historically and biblically based, Chad's book is an important and helpful addition in this sometimes neglected, but currently crucial area of our national life."

David L. Allen, dean
School of Theology
Southwestern Baptist Theological Seminary

"*Flourishing Faith* fills a desperately needed niche by providing a thoroughgoing survey of biblical and theological perspectives on work, wealth, government, and the economy. It will immediately become a classic text in this field, for I know of no one who can address these complex issues more articulately than Dr. Chad Brand."

Steve Lemke, provost
New Orleans Baptist Theological Seminary

"Chad Brand has provided readers with a helpful and informed survey of a broad array of interrelated themes, including work, wealth, stewardship, freedom, government, society, and church. Drawing upon the insights of historical theology and philosophy as well as economic and political theories, Brand weaves together big-picture ideas in a readable and understandable fashion for a wide audience. In doing so he articulates an economic philosophy shaped by baptistic expressions of the Christian tradition. Pastors, lay leaders, and students will receive wise guidance for wrestling with some of the most challenging issues of our twenty-first-century world."

David S. Dockery, president
Union University

"Dr. Brand has written a very helpful basic introduction to the history of the development of modern economic theories. In the process he helps explain why foundational Baptist beliefs are best reflected by a free-market system."

Richard Land, president
Ethics & Religious Liberty Commission
Southern Baptist Convention

FLOURISHING
FAITH

Primers in This Series

FLOURISHING FAITH

A Baptist Primer on Work, Economics, and Civic Stewardship

CHAD BRAND

With a Foreword by
Daniel L. Akin

Christian's LIBRARY PRESS

GRAND RAPIDS · MICHIGAN

ISBN 978-1-938948-15-2

Christian's Library Press
An imprint of the Acton Institute for the Study of Religion & Liberty
98 E. Fulton
Grand Rapids, Michigan 49503
www.clpress.com

Cover and interior design by Sharon VanLoozenoord
Editing by Stephen J. Grabill, Timothy J. Beals, and Paul J. Brinkerhoff

21 20 19 18 17 16 15 14 13   2 3 4 5 6 7 8 9 10

Printed in the United States of America
First edition

This book is
affectionately
dedicated to my wife

Tina Brand

You do so much
to make our life work,
and I love you!

Contents

Foreword

Al**l of us** have a worldview, a particular way of looking at, thinking about, and living life. It is a basic set of assumptions that gives meaning to our thoughts and actions. Christian author James Sire says, "A worldview is a commitment, a fundamental orientation of the heart, that can be expressed as a story or in a set of presuppositions (assumptions which may be true, partially true or entirely false) that we hold (consciously or subconsciously, consistently or inconsistently) about the basic constitution of reality, and that provides the foundation on which we live and move and have our being" (James W. Sire, *The Universe Next Door*, 5th ed., 20).

For a worldview to function properly, several characteristics must be present. It must be coherent and comprehensive, capable of addressing every aspect of life. It should shape our values and help us see what is important. It also should guide and influence our actions, assigning values and priorities to those actions. The comprehensive nature of a worldview is especially important when we consider the contours of this book.

You see, there is a Christian way to think about politics and economics. In fact we would be irresponsible to our Christian confession not to bring our Christian convictions to the table to determine how we should both think and act in these two important arenas of life. Living under the lordship of Jesus Christ means we "take every thought captive to obey Christ" (2 Cor. 10:5 ESV). That does mean everything.

Flourishing Faith by my good friend Chad Brand is a gold mine of wisdom and insight. It rightly notes the high calling of work and vocation that God gives to all who "image him." Further, Dr. Brand shows how the "work ethic" was passed on to America through the Reformers and Puritans, laying a foundation for the American experiment.

Now, where there is work there will be wealth, and the Bible speaks to this relationship as well. God is shown to be the maker of wealth, but in a fallen world the perpetual challenge is to use it well and wisely for the glory of God and the good of others. Dr. Brand will make the argument that this is best done by means of limited government and free enterprise. I believe he makes a very compelling argument.

At first blush you may think this book will be boring given the subject matter. You would be wrong. Chad Brand has a gift in taking a subject like economics and making it not just interesting, but extremely interesting. He is fair in his treatment of varying economic and political theories, but he also is clear where he stands and where he believes Scripture leads us. This is an excellent book. Read it with much profit.

Daniel L. Akin, president
Southeastern Baptist Theological Seminary
Wake Forest, NC

Introduction

In this primer, we are going to offer a brief examination of political economy in the Free Church or Baptist (or, baptist) tradition. By Free Church tradition I am referring to that group of churches that arose during and after the Reformation (sixteenth century) that rejected any direct linking with government. In Germany the Reform movement was led by stalwart professor Martin Luther, who then sought aid from the Duke of Saxony and other nobles to enable him to carry out this work. That aid was crucial to Luther's success. In the Swiss cities the reformations were instigated by magistrates who then enlisted the aid of teachers, pastors, theologians, and other persons with training in church and theology to help them carry them out. In England it was the king, Henry VIII, who sparked the new movement, and then placed individuals, especially Thomas Cranmer, in key places of leadership to ensure its success. Historians have labeled these Reform movements "Magisterial," since they worked in conjunction with magistrates or governments.

As early as the 1520s there were groups and individuals calling for reform who wanted those reforms carried out independent of magistrates. They recognized early on that if you get the government's help, you also reap its interference, and they were convinced that true reforms must be done according to the Word of God with no outside interference. The Swiss Brethren in Zurich were among the first of these groups, also known as "Anabaptists" (a term that has many difficulties), and we will tell a bit of their story in this volume. By the early 1600s English Separatists living in Holland came to affirm the same general approach, and the modern "Baptist" movement was founded. Over the intervening years many other groups came to affirm the same set of ideas: believer's baptism, local church autonomy, freedom from government intervention, and a regenerate church membership. Not all of them took the name "Baptist" (the general descriptor used in this book) but in principle they were baptistic, meaning that their unique theological identities coalesced around the previously mentioned set of ideas, hence the word, "baptist." Of course, in the last century or so, most "state-church" systems have been dismantled, or at least so modified that the state has little or no direct authority over denominations or churches anymore. Everyone from Dutch Calvinists to Roman Catholics has recognized this, but the pathway to that reality was long and hard fought, sometimes entailing people paying the ultimate sacrifice for their beliefs.

This book is one in a four-volume series on work, economics, and related issues and features contributions from four evangelical Protestant denominations: Baptist, Pentecostal, Reformed, and Wesleyan. In this book we will examine what I consider to be the five key issues related to political economy (a term we will define in the next chapter). Those issues are work (chaps. 1 and 2), wealth (chap. 3), government (chap. 4), and government taxation and its various implications (chap. 5); we will then consider an overall philosophy of how government relates to the entire structure and political economy (chap. 6); finally, we will offer a word about how Baptists have contributed to these issues and overall philosophy (chap. 7). Along the way I will also highlight the contributions of baptistic people, with the final chapter highlighting those contributions. They will not factor in heavily to every chapter since on some of these issues they made no *unique* contribution. But I think you will see that in some areas, Baptists made very important contributions that have led us to where we are in our world today.

I wish to clarify a couple of matters from the outset. One is the use of terminology in dealing with various philosophies of political economy. Though I do not take that topic up directly until chapter 6, I want to make clear where we are headed, up front. The word *capitalism* is often used in modern discourse to identify an approach to political economy clearly articulated in the late eighteenth century by Scottish philosopher and economist Adam Smith. Because the term has been saddled with a great deal of baggage (on all sides), we will generally use other terminology that clearly articulates what Smith had in mind (he never used the term *capitalism*) yet does not cause people's blood pressure to go up—on either side! The word *capitalism* was first used in the modern sense by Karl Marx, one of the founders of modern socialism. Marx saw the rise of industrial capitalism as class-based, and his rhetoric, especially in his magnum opus, *Das Kapital*, drove that class distinction. This, along with his basic philosophical belief, sometimes called *dialectical materialism*, resulted in a completely this-worldly and mechanical understanding of history and of the future of society. The debate over these issues through the centuries has not resulted in clarifying the terminological problem. So, we will try to avoid using terms and language that only muddy the water.

I am grateful to Stephen Grabill for the invitation to write this book, and to Stephen and to Chris Robertson for their excellent editorial assistance. I am also grateful to the Acton Institute for its incredible commitment to setting these issues before the public over many years. The Institute and its work are needed more than ever.

There are many people who have helped me along the years come to the place where I can offer some commentary on these matters. But the one person who has been my support through every single labor has been the love of my life, Tina Brand. It is to her that I lovingly dedicate this book.

"Workin' for a Livin'" | 1

An older American pop/rock band named Huey Lewis and the News had a hit song in 1982 called "Workin' for a Livin'." We prefer to add the final letter *g* to the two main words, but the idea expressed in the title of the song, that we are people who have to work for a living, expresses a basic biblical idea that is found over and over again in Scripture. And you might be surprised at what the Bible actually says about working for a living!

Before we explore the Bible's teaching about work, it might be helpful to set the historical context. The world into which Israel and then the church came was not a world that honored work, as Alvin Schmidt points out in his book, *How Christianity Changed the World*. The Greek philosopher Plato believed that manual work was to be done by slaves and the lower class of citizens, whom he called "bronze," in contrast to the "silver" administrative class and the "gold" ruling elite. To ask the upper two classes of society to do any kind of manual labor was, to Plato, *immoral*. The ancient philosopher and mathematician Archimedes was actually *ashamed* for having constructed devices that helped him work out geometry calculations, since it was beneath his dignity to work with his hands. Cicero, philosopher from Rome, complained that daily work of any kind was unbecoming to freeborn men. That was for slaves and slaves alone.

Both Greek and Roman societies were largely based on the economics of slavery, and the educated people of the time defended it. Aristotle argued that slavery was natural, expedient, and just. He believed that slaves were "living tools," and that a freeborn man could not be a friend with a slave *as* slave. Plato went so far as to defend the use of brutality against slaves when it was necessary, since in his view slaves were little more than brutes themselves. Most slaves in the Greco-Roman world were simply conquered peoples from nearby (usually non-Greek and non-Roman) countries. Ancient slavery was not usually race based. So, in the world that Westerners usually think of as the cradle of our philosophy and our culture, work, *manual labor* especially, was considered beneath a man's dignity, and was usually relegated to slaves or to the culturally lowest dregs of freemen. Labor was no activity for the educated and the cultured. Scripture, on the other hand, paints a very different picture.

We Were Created to Have Vocation

The story of human life in the Bible begins in a garden. Everything was perfect; there were no bad storms, no disease, no hunger, no dangerous animals, no pollution. The man and woman who were first created got along perfectly and had everything they needed. They even enjoyed fellowship with the Lord who made them, who came to them in a form they could see and with whom they could talk. They lived in what was, literally, a paradise. And yet in that paradise they were commanded to labor, to *work*!

Adam was given the daunting task of assigning names to all of the creatures (Gen. 2:19–20). Why did God not simply tell him what their names were? He could have done so, but he did not. The man had work to do. God commanded both the man and woman to "be fruitful and multiply; fill the earth and bring it under your dominion. Rule over the fish, the fowls, the beasts of the field. Bring all of the earth under your control" (Gen. 1:28–30, paraphrase). God made them in his image (Gen. 1:27). That meant perhaps many things, but one of the things it meant was that as God was Lord of all, so the humans would be lords (little *l*) over the earth. An ancient Near Eastern king would erect an image, a statue of himself, and place it on the highest spot in his land so the "image of the king" would cast his dominion far and wide. God's image would not be a *statue*—indeed, he would later explicitly prohibit the construction of any such image—but rather his image was the human beings that he himself had created. Abraham Kuyper once wrote that, "There is not a single square inch in the whole domain of our human existence over which Christ, who is sovereign over all, does not cry, 'Mine!'" In the creation of humans, that domain was delegated to the man and woman. They would be his image, his representatives on the earth, and they were intended to *flourish*.

Rule and subdue, tend and guard. These were their tasks. I agree with scholar Calvin Beisner who notes that these are two different functions: rule and subdue, tend and guard. To put it another way, our first parents were both to subject the world to their will and care for it at the same time. Later, as a result of the fall that came, these two tasks became confused. As a result there has been much confusion in history about the technological subjugation of the earth and the role of caring for the garden. But that confusion was not part of the original creation. They were to rule and subdue, tend and guard, and to do both with equal commitment.

That meant that they had work to do. Even as Yahweh had labored, creating the world in six days, so they would labor, as his representatives on the earth. And you have to remember that this was before the fall of man, the fall described in Genesis chapter 3. Work, in other words, is not a *result* of the fall into sin, but pre-dates that fall! I think we sometimes forget this fact and conclude that before sin entered the world, the man and woman frolicked around with little to do but laugh, play, and have a good time. But Scripture is clear that this was not so. Men and women were created, in part, to *work*. They were created for *more* than that; they were intended to employ their creative genius in understanding the world they were placed in, they were intended to mirror God's eternal triuneness in enjoying one another's fellowship, and they were intended to worship the One who had made them and placed them there. Yet they were created with the view that they had tasks to perform in this world, to make it into a better place, a well-tilled place, a managed place.

But then something happened; something that changed virtually everything. Eve was tempted by the serpent to do the one thing that God had prohibited them from doing: eating from the tree that is in "the midst of the garden." She succumbed to the temptation and offered the food to her husband, who also ate. The results were immediate and catastrophic.

God appeared and confronted the couple about their rebellion. After an indicting conversation, God then cursed the serpent, stating, among other things, that there would be continuous enmity between the serpent and his seed and the woman and her seed, seed that would eventually crush the head of the serpent (Gen. 3:15). He then told the woman that she would have increased pain in childbirth, and that her relationship with her husband would be altered. God then cursed the ground from which the man would extract those things that would make life livable, and that the nature of man's labor would now be severe and tedious in ways it would not have been before. He also informed the couple that because of their sin, that very ground that contained the treasures which God had created for the benefit of the humans he had made would be their eventual resting place, for "dust you are and to dust you will return" (Gen. 3:19). "Subduing" the earth just got a lot harder!

The Bible and the Way We Work

As the chapters of Genesis speed by, we find examples of those who use their God-given inventiveness to create tools and weapons, but then they use those very tools and weapons to rebel against God (Gen. 4:22–24). We see men gathering together in a city, Babel, where they will employ their labor to build a tower so that they might usurp God himself (Gen. 11). When we turn to the story of Jacob we find him working for his father-in-law, but both men employ deceitful tactics in the way they treat one another, with Laban changing Jacob's wages and Jacob attempting to change the makeup of Laban's flocks to his own benefit (Gen 30). Scripture teaches that honest weights and measures are to be used in financial transactions so neither businesses nor consumers would defraud one another (Lev. 19:35–36; Deut. 25:13–16; Prov. 11:1).

When we turn to the New Testament and to the narrative about Jesus, we find him being born into a very humble family of people. Jesus' stepfather, Joseph, was a "carpenter" (Matt. 13:55), and though that term may not denote exactly the same occupation that it does today, it is clear that he labored with his hands in intractable materials, apparently wood. Jesus is also called "the carpenter" (Mark 6:3), and so it would appear that he labored alongside Joseph in his work. Perhaps they had a small shop, or it may be that they worked as builders of some sort, but the point is that Jesus was a *laboring* man. Because Joseph is never mentioned in the Gospels after Jesus grew to manhood, some have speculated that he may have died when Jesus was young, leaving us with the impression that Joseph's oldest "son" carried on his father's trade and so cared for the family, perhaps alongside his younger brothers. The second-century writer Justin Martyr presents Jesus "working as a carpenter when among men, making yokes and ploughs; by which he taught the symbols of righteousness and an active life." It is not clear how Justin knew this much, and it may have been speculation, but the basic story is upheld by the Gospels.

Jesus believed in work! In his parables he often spoke of work, and spoke of it as an honorable thing. He told of a man working in a field and also of a pearl merchant, both professions (Matt. 13:44–45). He exemplified fishermen working with nets (Matt. 13:47–48), and fishing in those days was not for relaxation but for earning one's living. He related a tale of a man sowing seed in a field, planting his crops (Mark 4:10–20), and of a man who owned a field that had a weed problem (Matt. 13:24–30). He told of shepherds who labored hard and faithfully so as not to lose any of the sheep that their employers owned (Luke 15:1–7). Jesus uttered some parables that seem to have rather odd and even unjust implications when it comes to working. The parable of the ten minas (Luke 19:11–27) has a businessman going on a long trip and leaving his fortune in the hands of ten servants. Some of the servants made good investments with their master's money, and when he returned he rewarded them. But one servant simply hid the money away so as not to lose it, and the master had harsh words (and more) for that servant. In the parable of the workers in the vineyard, men were hired at various times of the day, and they all went out and worked and received the pay that was due them (Matt. 20:1–16; more on this parable in chapter 3). I realize that these parables are not primarily about work and that they each have a point to make in Jesus' teaching on the kingdom. But it is clear from these texts that Jesus believed in labor and elevated laborers often to a high status as examples of the kingdom he came to bring.

In the New Testament epistles, Paul instructed the Thessalonians to be hardworking people. He makes clear that generosity toward the truly needy is important, but if able-bodied men will not work, they should not be given church welfare. "If a man won't work, he shall not eat" (2 Thess. 3:10, paraphrase). This is so lazy and unproductive people will not be encouraged to "walk in a disorderly manner" (v. 11). When you work, whatever the work is (even the work of slaves), you should do it "unto the Lord" (Col. 3:23). To slaves he wrote that they should obey their masters "like slaves of Christ, doing the will of God from your heart" (Eph. 6:5–6). He then enjoins masters to treat their slaves in a just and honorable manner, remembering that "he who is both their Master and yours is in heaven" and that he sees both masters and slaves in the same way (Eph. 6:9; cf. Philem. 16).

These were not idle words from the apostle, who himself earned his own way during much of his ministry, even though he knew that he had a right to depend on the gifts of the churches for his support (1 Thess. 2:9; 1 Cor. 9:14–15). In a later letter he made it clear that he would not "take advantage" of his position in ministry by expecting the Corinthians to provide his living, but instead worked with his own hands (2 Cor. 12:16–17). Even though Jesus had taught that those who minister should receive support from those they served, "for the worker is worth his keep" (Matt. 10:10, as quoted by Paul in 1 Tim. 5:18), and though Paul noted that even the oxen are not muzzled when treading the grain (also 1 Cor. 9:9 from Deut. 25:4), he set the example by laboring for his keep while in Corinth and other places of ministry. The New Testament is as clear as the Old Testament that work is honorable, and that it is a necessary part of life. It is also clear that work ought to be done honestly, with a whole heart, unto the Lord. Furthermore, while Jesus criticizes some rich "employers" in his parables for their materialism (Luke 12:13–21; 16:19–31), he praises other rich men for their honesty and justice (Matt. 18:21–35; 20:1–16).

Being an *entrepreneur*, like the man in the parable of the workers and the vineyard is completely consistent with being a faithful disciple of the Lord, as long as one treats workers, wealth, and the Lord in ways that are pleasing to God. Those who have people in their employ should treat their workers with respect and honor, and give to them their just deserts for their service.

Conclusion

The Bible elevates work to a very high position of prominence, making it clear that humans were created to work, as well as to worship, have families, understand their world, and exercise dominion over it. That very command from Genesis 2, to exercise dominion over the world, demands that people find a *way* to do so. That is, they have to find a way of working in the world. The kinds of work that people do will of course vary. Some find joy in laboring with their hands while others find every bit as much joy in laboring with their minds, or in a thousand other ways. The notion that work was simply a by-product of the fall of humanity into sin is simply not sustainable. And, since the eternal destiny of humans will be to live on a "new earth" for eternity (Rev. 21–22), that is, in the *world*, not in some ethereal, heavenly, vaguely defined existence, it is also likely that they will have tasks to do there—for eternity! That will be work with the complete absence of drudgery.

Let's turn our attention now to how certain people in the history of the church have worked out some of these ideas.

Study Questions

1. Our study pointed out that Adam and Eve were created, at least in part, to work even before they fell into sin. What are the

implications of God commanding work in advance of the fall, if any, for Christian vocation, both in this age and in the age to come?

2. How were Adam and Eve, before the fall into sin, intended to combine the tasks of dominion over creation and at the same time tending to it? What complications entered after they sinned?

3. How do the examples Jesus used in his parables illustrate for us his own attitudes toward working people? How should we incorporate those ideas into our own understanding of work?

For Further Reading

Beisner, E. Calvin. *Where Garden Meets Wilderness.* Grand Rapids: Eerdmans, 1997.

Kuyper, Abraham. "Sphere Sovereignty." In *Abraham Kuyper: A Centennial Reader*, ed. James D. Bratt. Grand Rapids: Eerdmans, 1998.

Schmidt, Alvin J. *How Christianity Changed the World.* Grand Rapids: Zondervan, 2004.

A Theology of Work | 2

In the previous chapter we saw how Scripture teaches the value of work, all kinds of work, from laboring to managing, from relatively poor people sweating it out on a farm in the hot summer sun to capital-rich entrepreneurs building prosperous businesses that can then employ other people, sometimes *lots* of other people. We wish to develop these ideas further in this chapter by giving an overview of some key moments in the history of Christianity and demonstrating how Christian thinkers developed a *theology of work*. The concept of a *theology* of work may be new to you, but this is exactly what will take shape by the end of the chapter. Also note how this theology will eventually integrate what we might call the *individual* aspect with the *social* aspect. At the individual level there is labor, something that you or I do to make a living. But if we expand that out, if we raise the camera up high enough to take a look at all of Kentucky (where I live) or even all of America and look at that labor in the larger picture, then we are looking not at one person working, but at the *economy*.

That is not a scary word. It comes from the Greek word *oikonomia*, which means "the law of the house." To look at the economy in this way requires us to think about how the parts work together to make a whole. Now you can do that in a college course on macro-economics, but we are going to try to do something of that here by looking at how Christians through history have developed an understanding of economics, starting first with an individual theology of work and then expanding that out to the larger picture. In some sense it will take the rest of this book to finish this task, but in this chapter we will look at this developing theology of how we ought to carry out our calling or work before God.

Working for a Living in Early Christianity

Work is sometimes difficult (remember, "by the sweat of your brow"), and there is no doubt about that. Yet, work we must in spite of the difficulty. And that work takes place in a fallen world where we often have to work right alongside others who have not been redeemed—and there are good reasons why we should work alongside such persons! Let's see how the church over time worked out a Christian understanding of work.

In the early days of Christianity the church was under fire. Christians gave their sole allegiance to Christ as Lord, but this commitment came into conflict with the demands of the Roman government that the empire itself be recognized as divine. This eventually led to the exaltation of the emperors themselves to the status of gods, and citizens of the empire were expected to render worship to them publicly. The Jewish nation was granted an exemption from this expectation, but in return it was expected to be obedient to Roman governance. The early Christians, though, were not confined to a single national identity, and their unwillingness to worship Rome brought them into conflict with governing authorities very early, with notable martyrdoms occurring throughout the second century. By the third century the emperors began to issue general orders for enforced sacrifices on an empire-wide basis. Thousands of Christians died and others endured horrible persecution. But early in the fourth century (AD 313) the emperor Constantine issued the Edict of Milan, effectively ending the persecutions, and he also endorsed the Christian faith. In 381, Emperor Theodosius outlawed all pagan religions, essentially making Christianity the official religion of the Roman Empire.

That's a good thing, right? Well, let's look a little closer. Now with Christianity legal, socially acceptable, and eventually the official religion of state, everybody wanted to get in on it. By the middle of the fifth century there would be nearly universal infant baptism in the Roman Empire, making almost everyone a "Christian." But were they all really? The obvious answer is, "No!" As might be expected, in the midst of this "dumbing down" of the expectations for what it means to be a Christian, protest movements arose. One of the most prominent forms of protest would take the form of what we call "monasticism."

The earliest "monastics" (the word comes from the Greek, *monachos*, which means, "alone") were hermits, known as "anchorites," and they were men, like Anthony of Egypt, who fled to the desert to spend their time in solitude, praying and engaging in spiritual warfare. Later, monastic communities formed. The most prominent of these in the first millennium of the church formed around the work of an Italian monk named Benedict. The Benedictine monasteries would grow over time, till there were literally thousands of them dotting the European landscape. Monks took a vow of poverty, chastity, and obedience, and over time the theology of monasticism came to insist that the monastery was the one place where a Christian could live out a holy calling; in fact, it was the only place where one could do so, out of the rough and tumble of the sort of moral and spiritual compromises that were a part of the everyday life of farmers, soldiers, merchants, and noblemen. Only the monks were truly "called" by God to this vocation of service. All others lived relatively tainted lives that entailed a certain amount of compromise with the world.

After Rome: Brave New World

With this is mind, one of the oddest developments in the centuries after the fall of the Roman Empire (the last emperor was deposed in 476) was the rise of what can only be called "Catholic capitalism." Rome was an empire whose economy was largely (though not exclusively) slave-driven. When more labor was needed to work in farming, domestic employment, or even tasks such as medicine, the Romans went to war with one of the neighboring "barbaric" nations, and brought war captives back to the provinces to supply the needed labor pool. When a state has a ready reserve of slave labor to solve its problem of the need for a work force, it has little incentive to seek out other types of solutions to solve those problems. So, in the period of empire (roughly 27 BC to AD 476), people in the Roman Empire invented virtually no new technologies. Europeans in the year AD 500 used essentially the same kinds of wagons, plows, ships, harnesses, weapons, farming techniques, and blacksmithing that they had used a thousand years earlier.

Over the next three centuries or so all of that would change. Enterprising people who now needed machines to help them do more work in the absence of a ready-made slave labor force would invent the waterwheel, the horse collar (and ways to harness horses or oxen side by side), rudders for ships, the stirrup, wagons with tongues that could swivel, and many other devices to make transportation, manufacturing, and fighting more efficient. Before the waterwheel mill (or the windmill in some places) all manufacturing and winnowing had to be done by hand; now a shaft turned by water or wind currents could assist in the work. Before the rudder, ships had to be turned by banks of rowers on either side of the ship; now a single pilot operating a tiller or a wheel could do the same work alone. Before the stirrup, there was no place for heavy cavalry in battle who could attack an enemy in a charge with lance or spear; now a mounted horseman with heavy gear could unhorse an opposing horseman without fear that his attack would actually knock him off his own horse.

This latter technology, the stirrup, was likely employed in one of the most important battles in history, the Battle of Tours in France in AD 732, and then again four years later at the Battle of Narbonne, as the Frankish army of Charles Martel defeated invading Muslim forces whose horses were not outfitted with stirrups. Martel's cavalry prevailed in both instances, since the Muslim horsemen were no match for these men who had stability on their mounts. Had Martel lost these battles, we might have all grown up reading the "King James Version" of the Qur'an! These technological developments, and scores of others over the following centuries (the compass, gunpowder, mechanical clocks, etc.) would radically change the way people worked and fought, and would eventually result in the West gaining significant advantages over the rest of the world.

So, what about those Catholic capitalists? German sociologist Max Weber wrote a book in 1904 and 1905 that became famous: *The Protestant Ethic and the Spirit of Capitalism*. In that book, Weber argued that the philosophical underpinnings that underlay the development of and intellectual support for the entrepreneurial spirit in the modern world were laid by the Protestant Reformers of the sixteenth century, especially John Calvin. Historically speaking there is something to that, but it is clear to us now that Weber's claim was both overstated and not always based on the actual facts of Western economic or churchly development. In other words, entrepreneurialism was in the world *long* before Calvin taught the importance of work and thrift, and those who followed his teaching in this area were not all morbid "capitalists" who spent their days counting receipts and worrying about their souls, as Weber had argued. He claimed that Calvin and later the Puritans had inadvertently constructed an "iron cage" of consumption, selfishness, greed, and other unsavory characteristics that he (Weber) believed were endemic in their whole understanding of work, wealth, and government. In developing his treatment in this way, Weber was attempting to label all of the dark features of industrialization (long work hours, child labor, fetid work conditions) as being an outcome of a dreary Calvinistic and Puritan vision of life. I am convinced that Weber was wrong at many points of his analysis, helpful though his work has been in some ways. What is also important to note, as we will see in what follows, is that a real entrepreneurial spirit had emerged in the world long *before* Calvin was born. It developed, of all places, in Catholic monasticism, that one institution where the brothers all took vows of "poverty."

Remember that the monks took a vow of *obedience* as well as a vow of poverty and chastity. It was a vow of obedience to the brothers in the monastery, and it entailed manual labor, among other things. The monasteries planted vineyards and other crops and raised horses, cattle, and sheep. Early on this was done for the purpose of subsistence, but over time they found ways to be very efficient at what they were doing. They made use of the new inventions already mentioned as well as new methods of farming, moving from a two-field system to a three-field system, a move that enabled them to yield about 35 percent greater harvests than before.

These men had no wives, no children, and lots of time and energy on their hands! Monasteries made money by saying masses for the wealthy, and often these funds were used to purchase land, and later more land. One monastery in Hungary in the eighth century had 250,000 acres under plow. Many had in excess of 100,000 acres. They bred some of the best horses in Europe at the time, and eventually delved into a variety of different businesses, even banking. Of course, all profits accrued to the monastic community since no monk could own anything. The fascinating thing about this story is that it makes clear that the first entrepreneurs in the Western world were not Dutch bankers, Venetian ship builders, or Genevan merchants, but Catholic monks! And of course, they believed, as their system had taught them, that the only truly holy people, the only ones with a real calling, were those who had separated themselves into monastic communities. But that idea was about to be challenged.

All Have a Vocation

In 1517 an Augustinian monk in Saxony (Germany) sparked off a theological debate that grew into the movement we now call the Protestant Reformation. Luther's major slogan was "justification by faith alone," but a corollary of that, and a point Luther made with almost as much ferocity as he did justification, was the idea that all Christians have a vocation (*vocatio* in Latin), that all Christians are divinely *called*. Whether one is a farmer, a banker, a scholar, a priest, or a merchant, Luther believed that all are callings from God and that the calling to a "secular" vocation is just as holy as a calling to a "sacred" vocation. Indeed, the distinction between sacred and secular becomes very *blurred* in Luther's theology. In effect, this notion of vocation did more to elevate the field of "business" than anyone might have thought possible. R. H. Murray in his book, *The Political Consequences of the Reformation*, offered this comment: "The 'Saint's Rest' was in the world to come: in this [world] he was to labor at his calling. Business henceforth became a sacred office in which it was man's bounden duty to do his utmost *ad majorem Dei gloriam* [to the greatness of God's glory]." Labor glorifies God, and it is in that sense that every calling is a calling from God. In Catholicism the workplace could *not* have been seen as sacred (at that time), since only the communion of the saints in heaven is sacred. Luther had brought heaven down to earth.

Connected to this is Luther's doctrinal conviction that all Christians are *priests* unto God (1 Peter 2:9). Luther did not diminish the importance of the role of "pastor," but instead leveled the playing field, making that calling but *one* calling in the life of Christian people. All believers are priests, which means that all believers have the responsibility of serving one another in ministry. This preaching did not have the immediate effect of harnessing a vast lay movement toward ministry, but in the generations that followed a movement in Lutheranism called Pietism would seize on these ideas and witness a lay revival movement that empowered people in "secular" employment to use their gifts and callings to serve the church. Luther's doctrine of the priesthood of all believers would also spill over into later Baptist and Methodist circles, evangelical denominations that emphasized even more than Lutheranism that all are called into God's service.

Luther's reform initiative would eventually swallow up large parts of Western Europe (including England) after his public stand before the emperor and the papacy at the Diet (Congress) of Worms in 1521. There, Luther, in defiance of the established powers in his part of the world proclaimed, "Here I stand. I cannot do otherwise. God help me. Amen." The Reformation was on, and it would, over time, completely transform the way Europeans thought about church, theology, politics, and work.

Vocation from Geneva to Cane Ridge

Two decades after Luther sparked the revolt that we call the Reformation, a Frenchman named John Calvin was working to help reform the churches in the Swiss city of Geneva. (He arrived in 1536.) The town council there had forced the Catholic bishop out, and, for mostly political and economic reasons, set about the task of de-Catholicizing the city, hiring Calvin to take the lead in carrying out that difficult task. Calvin's reforms were root and branch; not merely theological and ecclesiastical, they covered every area from politics to economics to cultural and moral life and more.

Calvin's theology emphasized the doctrine of depravity (sin), and Calvin knew that sloth and envy were still dangers facing regenerate people. Therefore, pastors and peers needed to encourage people to work, and to work hard (see David W. Hall and Matthew D. Burton, *Calvin and Commerce*). Calvin once wrote, "Sloth and selfishness, in the changed universe, have become more normal than industry and stewardship." Because of this, a work ethic is required of us. In addition, individuals will seldom work hard for nothing, and it is also tempting to slack off if we have already been paid for a job that is not yet complete, so employers should be encouraged to pay good wages, but to proffer payment only *after* a job is complete. For the Genevan Reformer, all of life is to be lived to the glory of God, and that includes the way one carried out his life of working.

The real heirs to Calvin's views on these kinds of issues were the Puritans, and especially the American Puritans. Arriving in New England aboard the *Arbella* in 1630, John Winthrop proclaimed that he and those with him were about to establish "a city upon a hill." Fleeing King Charles's persecutions of the Puritan party in the Anglican Church, they had come to the New World with very specific convictions about worship, life, and work. In England, work was often viewed by the elites as something not for *gentlemen*, a belief that we have already seen in classical authors. Thomas More had written a book called *Utopia* a century earlier, a book about what life might be like in America, and in that book he depicted Englishmen doing *some* work in the New World, but not much, and only for the purpose of self-discipline, not for personal satisfaction or to be of service to others. Real gentlemen need intellectual activity, pleasant discourse, and leisure, and work interferes with all of those activities.

Pioneering Puritan theologians in England had rejected such notions. William Perkins of Cambridge had written that "Adam in his innocence had all things at his will, yet then God employed him in a calling." Work was a means of fulfillment for Perkins, not punishment. He also contended that there is no distinction between manual labor and other activities, whether vocational or aesthetic. Cotton Mather, a third-generation Puritan in America, wrote, "Oh, let every Christian walk with God when he works at his calling, act with cooperation with an eye to God, act as under the eye of God." God looks at the heart of the worker, not the *kind* of work he does. For Mather, work was not an imposition of society, but a divine vocation.

This conviction resulted in remarkable success for the New England colony. Perry Miller, noted historian of the American Puritans, referred to their mission to America as "An Errand in the Wilderness." Virginia was the place that had *seemed* to promise quick economic returns, with its rich Chesapeake soil perfect for growing tobacco and other important crops. Cold and rocky Massachusetts was not promising. By 1624, though, Virginia, which began as a joint-stock corporation, had become "a royal Crown colony after the failure of the profit-sharing arrangements between investors and settlers and the use of land grants to attract labor," in the words of economics and history professors Stanley L. Engerman and Robert H. Gallman. Early Virginia settlers were not passionate about faith and family, as the New Englanders were.

In Massachusetts they worked very hard and found that timber (for a lumber hungry England), fishing (especially cod), farming (once they had learned how to adjust to the harsh climate), fur-trading, and other industries were available to them, and that by hard work, thrift, and generosity, they could build for themselves a thriving civilization. This all made New England a wealthy colony in less time than anyone would have thought possible. But it was their faith that drove them on, their belief that God had sent them to this place, and the encouragement of godly pastors and godly magistrates to honor God, to love their families, and to work hard for God's glory.

Of course, this was only the beginning. Over the next three and a half centuries America would become the pacesetter in the world in terms of fruitful output. During the Revolutionary War that began in 1775, American industry surged forward to provide all the things needed to supply their military forces against the British. As the war ended Americans rushed down the Ohio River valley and over the Cumberland Gap to settle in Kentucky, Indiana, and Tennessee, exercising dominion over a whole new vista of lands that seemed almost unending. As the nineteenth century dawned, daring individuals streamed across the Mississippi River and found the fertile fields of Missouri and Arkansas waiting for their plows. New technologies of the time—the John Deere steel plowshare, the McCormick reaper, and others—made it possible to turn these untilled lands whose prairie grass roots plunged eighteen inches into the soil, a depth that would have made them impenetrable without the new technologies.

Across the Alleghenies in 1801 revival broke out in a place called Cane Ridge in Bourbon County, Kentucky (see John B. Boles, *The Great Revival*). Assorted Baptists, Methodists, and Presbyterians witnessed thousands of conversions in what was in effect the first massive spiritual awakening in the South. Out of this and subsequent "camp meetings," the Baptists and Methodists would grow to be the two largest denominations in America by 1850, though they were tiny in 1800. The primary approach to ministry by the Baptists was the farmer-preacher. Evangelists would come and found a church in a small community in Kentucky or Tennessee and then would move on, appointing one of the farmers who could read and who appeared to have a "call to preach" to carry on as pastor. Such men rarely had any kind of formal training in the early years, but they knew they had been called to preach even as they had been called to farm, and the Puritan and Reformation principle of "vocation" applied to them in more ways than one.

America as the Engine of Vocation

By the time of the Civil War there were over 150,000 manufacturing facilities in America, most of them in the North, a fact that made the war all the more challenging for the agrarian South. Railroads had sprung up in the 1820s, and within a few years after the end of the Civil War, a transcontinental railroad reduced travel time across the American continent to a matter of days, rather than the months it had required previously. All of this happened because of American fruitfulness. An American congressman made these points in a speech given in 1846: "I invite you to go to the west, and visit one of our log cabins, and number its inmates. There you will find a strong, stout youth of eighteen, with his Better Half, just commencing the first struggle of independent life. Thirty years from that time, visit them again; and instead of two, you will find in that same family twenty-two. That is what I call the American Multiplication Table." The 1800 census had American population at 5.3 million, but by 1820 that number had increased to 9.6 million, at a time when immigration rates were very low.

Americans who wanted to become successful had few obstacles but natural ones. The intractability of the soil, the dangers of travel to the open west, the daunting task of settling land, stretching fences, building a house, hunting for food—these were their challenges, and they could be overwhelming. But they were not the same challenges that faced the average European. Back on the Continent the dominance of trade guilds made occupational relocation almost impossible. In many European countries one needed government approval even to change jobs. Available land had long since been occupied, and it was difficult, often impossible, to buy property, even if one had money. Ancient customs and traditions locked people into the same kind of life, status, and career that had been part of the family experience for generations. This was not the case in America, and the founding documents of this country made essential freedoms, the kinds of freedoms one needs to find maximum fruitfulness, available to nearly all persons.

Nearly all, but not all. Slaves imported from Africa and their descendants did not have those freedoms until after the Civil War, and even then, bigotry, Jim Crow laws, so-called Southern "Redemption," and discrimination prohibited most blacks from realizing the "American Dream" for another century. Native Americans were herded around to reservations and kept out of the American hope for many decades. Women did not have the right to vote or even to work in the way men did until the early twentieth century. With those exceptions in mind, however, America was still a place where people could find a way to work their way into prosperity, and for the most part, they did. In a sense, the theology of Luther, Calvin, Perkins, and the early Baptist farmer-preachers would see its fruition in the powerful industrial giant that became twentieth-century America.

Conclusion

In this chapter we have tried to examine the issue of *working*. The Scriptures elevate human labor of all kinds to a laudable, fulfilling, and God-honoring calling. Although the church has not always seen work as occupying an important place in life, the Reformers and the Puritans in keeping with Scripture made it clear that all people have a calling and that all believers are priests unto the Lord. As the Puritans made their way to America, they came to a place in the world where they could put their theology of work into practice, virtually unimpeded by law, tradition, or custom, and that in doing so they found incredible success. Though the record is mixed, for the most part, America became the testing ground for the Reformation theology of work that has proved amazingly fruitful, even where the people who found that success were themselves not Christian believers. While Christian teachers such as Luther, Calvin, Perkins, and Mather developed a theology for how people work, they did not develop a coherent *theory* of economics. They did not take the step we identified earlier in this chapter of relating the individual (labor) to the social (economy), except at small and local levels, such as the city of Geneva or the townships of Massachusetts. This individual-social or labor-economy connection will come later in chapters 6 and 7.

Having developed a theology of work, we will next attempt to work out a theology of wealth to see what end result can come from human fruitfulness done for the glory of God.

Study Questions

1. If you had to state a *theology of work* in five or six sentences, what would you say?

2. How does the Catholic combination of monastic seclusion accompanied by a strong focus on working compare to the Protestant and Puritan work ethic?

3. Summarize John Calvin's and Martin Luther's theology of work.

4. How has America in its history demonstrated the value of and the truthfulness of the biblical teachings on people having a calling, working hard, and being creative?

5. In light of what we have discussed in this chapter, is it better to be a manual laborer, a minister, a business owner, or a teacher? Why?

For Further Reading

Bainton, Roland. *Here I Stand: A Life of Martin Luther.* Nashville: Abingdon, 1950.

Boles, John B. *The Great Revival, 1787–1805: The Origins of the Southern Evangelical Mind.* Lexington: University Press of Kentucky, 1972.

Engerman, Stanley L., and Robert H. Gallman. "The Emergence of a Market Economy before 1860." In *A Companion to 19th-Century America.* Edited by William L. Barney. Malden, MA: Blackwell, 2006.

Hall, David W., and Matthew D. Burton. *Calvin and Commerce: The Transforming Power of Calvinism in Market Economics.* Phillipsburg, NJ: P&R, 2009.

Stark, Rodney. *The Victory of Reason: How Christianity Led to Freedom, Capitalism, and Western Success.* New York: Random House, 2005.

Wealth | 3

John Kenneth Galbraith, a well-known economist, wrote many books, but the one that has the most arresting title is simply called *Money*. (It does also have a subtitle: *Whence It Came, Where It Went*.) Money is funny. Most of us probably think we know exactly what money is, since all our lives we have gone shopping and just handed over cash and coins (or in more recent years, swiped our card) and gotten whatever we purchased. There it is in our wallet or purse; it is just *money*! And we need to talk a bit about money, but only as a prelude to talking about something more important—*wealth*!

In the history of the world, money has been very different from what it is today. In the ancient Roman world, many things were used as mediums of exchange, including things like *salt*. The Native Americans in New York (or New Holland, early on) used pieces of glass or beads to trade with the Dutch (and later, English) traders who came in search of furs. This "wampum" as it was called was very easy for the Dutch to come by (easier than gold!), but it became a medium of exchange *among* the Indians as they bartered for goods with one another and with the Europeans. Coins made of precious metals were first introduced in the Mediterranean world around the year 600 BC, and were considered to be of value because they actually *had* value as precious metals. Even before that, precious metals were used in the form of rings or other shapes before coinage was instituted. Paper money is of much more recent invention and only has value so long as the government issuing it (and merchants who receive it) recognizes it as *legal tender*. Monopoly money will not get you very much stuff at Walmart or McDonalds!

My purpose in this chapter is not to give you a history of money but to talk about what Scripture and the Christian tradition have had to say about how we put it to use. To put it in a bit larger and broader perspective, what does the Bible say about *wealth*? What is wealth? Is it biblically legitimate to accumulate wealth? What kinds of things should we do with our wealth? Is there such a thing as a *theology of wealth* much like a theology of work, which we developed in the last chapter? These are the questions we wish to explore in this chapter, so let's get to it.

Money and Wealth in the Bible

The first thing to note is that God himself created wealth. He did so in the creation of the earth and the cosmos itself. God invested in this world more abundance of good things than we are ever likely to fathom. Think of the vast array of natural resources that are here in our world, from timber to ore to a plentitude of animal and plant life. There is gold in mountains and rivers, iron in deposits literally all over the world, animals to be harnessed, fish to be caught and eaten, coal deposits that have fueled the Industrial Revolution, and, of immense benefit to humanity for the last 150 years, oil and natural gas in the ground. Who knows how many quadrillions (or far more!) of dollars' worth of resources are to be found in the land beneath our feet and in the mountains and trees that soar over our heads? And it is all here because a rich God put it in place for our use!

One of the first wealthy people we encounter in the Bible is also a man extolled both in the Genesis story and later in the New Testament as a man of faith: Abraham. He was a man who, by the time he had followed the Lord's direction to move to Canaan, "had become very wealthy in livestock and in silver and gold" (Gen. 13:2). Abraham's wealth was a blessing from God, and he used his wealth to be a blessing to other people in his day. Abraham *flourished*, and helped others to flourish as well. Other prominent wealthy people in Scripture include Caleb, who in courage and faith in God conquered a large territory in the land of Canaan and commanded much property (Josh. 15). The kings of Israel, especially David and Solomon were wealthy men by virtue of their positions as king and through their capable administrations. Job was a wealthy man before his troubles befell him, and after the loss of everything the Lord restored to him double of what he had lost (Job 42:10). The list of what he owned makes it clear that Job was not just wealthy, but *massively* wealthy: the Bill Gates of his time! Joseph of Arimathea in the New Testament was also a man of property who used his wealth to provide burial for the Lord after his crucifixion (Matt. 27:57–59). These men were wealthy and yet, overall, were faithful to God, though in the case of Solomon his wealth in some ways diverted his faithfulness in his later years.

There were also wealthy men who were *not* faithful to God. Nabal was a wealthy man in David's day, yet he refused to render service to the fleeing David in his need (1 Sam. 25). Ahab was a king of Israel who had great wealth, but when he coveted another man's vineyard, he and his murderous wife plotted against the man, had him killed, and the king then seized the land (1 Kings 21). Here is

Ahab adding to his wealth by *extraction*, not by production. He saw something he wanted, a vineyard, and he used his coercive powers as king to take it. This brought about moral decay in the land and the condemnation of the prophet Elijah, who denounced Ahab's actions: "Have you not murdered a man and seized his property?" (1 Kings 21:19). In the New Testament there are several examples of wicked men who are also rich, including Annas the chief priest and various governing dignitaries in the book of Acts. The rich young man who encountered Jesus balked when the Lord told him to sell what he had and give it to the poor, preferring his wealth to following Jesus (Mark 10:17–31). The point here is that wealth in and of itself appears neither to be a good thing nor a bad thing in Scripture; everything depends on *what* one does with one's riches and on *how* that wealth is procured. Work (to tie in with the previous chapters) creates wealth both for individuals (labor) and for entire societies (economies), but wealth created by theft or governmental extraction creates moral *decay* that can be seen in individual lives and in broader social institutions.

Jesus came into a world dominated by power politics and by greed for wealth (see Alan B. Wheatley, *Patronage in Early Christianity*). The leaders of Israel, among whom were the Sadducees, were people who had sidled up to the Roman occupiers and had become wealthy in return. There was a patron-client relationship throughout much of the Roman Empire at that time, with wealthy patrons (Roman elites) utilizing provincial clients in various parts of the empire in order to keep the people in check. The "clients" in Judea were largely the priestly class. The coming of Jesus made them fearful that somehow he might incite the people into some kind of rebellion, and that "the Romans will come and take away both our place [the temple] and our nation" (John 11:48–50). It was this concern, for their position and possessions, that led to their plot to assassinate Jesus. In the long run they did lose their place and their nation (and their wealth) in AD 70 when Emperor Titus destroyed Jerusalem and its temple, but none of this was Jesus' fault. In first-century Palestine (the Roman name for Judea), the wealthy class made up about 10 percent of the population, with the rest consisting of the poor or the very poor. There was only a very small "middle class" of artisans, shopkeepers, fishermen, and so on in that day. So then, what did Jesus himself teach about wealth?

In the Sermon on the Mount (Matt. 5–7), Jesus instructs his hearers on what the "blessed life" actually is. In a truly counter-cultural manner, he says nothing to them about a life filled with financial rewards. In fact, he begins with, "Blessed are the poor in spirit for theirs is the kingdom of heaven" (Matt. 5:3). Note well that he is not speaking about *financial* poverty here but about *spiritual* poverty. "Blessed are they who recognize their spiritual poverty before God." That seems to be the gist of what he is saying as Matthew conveys Jesus' teaching to us (cf. Luke 6:20). People who have that kind of attitude will receive the reward of eternal life. In fact, most of the Sermon on the Mount addresses the issue of what our attitudes ought to be on a variety of matters, such as vengeance, the taking of oaths, our married life, giving alms, public prayer, fasting, and other things that are a part of everyday life—that part of our existence that can get mired down in compromise and complacency. In our relationships with others it is crucial that we do not seek reciprocity, or tit for tat, whether it is in financial matters, vengeance, retaliation toward those who have wronged us, or any other area of life (Matt. 5:21–48).

In Matthew chapter 6, as Jesus continues his address, he gets to the issue of treasures and troubles. He instructs his hearers to "store up for yourselves treasures in heaven, where moth and rust do not destroy, and where thieves do not break in and steal" (Matt. 6:19–24). Jesus is not teaching that money (treasure) is irrelevant or of no importance in this life. He is teaching us that we need to set priorities in life, and that serving the Lord (storing up treasures in heaven) ought to be our first priority. People need money for their daily living (as he makes clear in the next paragraph), but we ought not to "treasure" tangible things unduly. It is important to remember at this point that most people who "love" money do not generally love money itself; they love what money can do for them, like buying nice things or taking expensive trips. That is, they enjoy *wealth*, as we have been arguing all along. People with misplaced values in this area generally love the prestige that accrues to them from others because they can buy a Porsche or a vacation home in Florida or designer clothing. Poor people struggle with the same temptation, the difference being that their "status symbols" (for example, cable or satellite TV, large screen plasma TV, video game systems) will be less expensive, but often no less *important*. This too is what Jesus is warning against. "Where your treasure is, there your heart will be also." In other words, our heart follows our treasure, not the other way around. The important thing is to "treasure" the right things so that our "heart" will be in the right place.

In the next paragraph (Matt. 6:25–34), Jesus enjoins his hearers (and us, by extension) not to be filled with *anxiety* over whether we will have the goods that are necessary to live. He informs them that God cares for things like birds and plants, and if so, he will also provide for us. It is important not to misunderstand Jesus here. Someone might read this text and conclude that this means he or she does not need to get a job and work, since, after all, God will take care of us. Consider the example Jesus gives: birds.

I love to watch birds (though I am not, technically, a "bird watcher"). I live in a partially wooded area and I love to sit on my deck with a glass of iced tea and watch the birds, squirrels, and other creatures all around. One thing I have noticed about birds is that they are almost constantly active during daylight hours. They are flying around, looking for bugs and seeds (or rabbits and other birds, for the raptors) in order to feed themselves and their young. They don't sit on a fence with their beaks open waiting for God to *drop* something in. (My four cockatiels in the cage in my study are the exception; every morning when I wake up and they hear me walking, they start squawking for food—welfare birds!) So what does Jesus mean here? He means that God has given us an abundantly gifted world in which to live and work, a world filled with all of the abundance of things we need to make our way in life and to *flourish*. That includes tangible things like fish and game, but it also includes intangible things like *opportunities*. The Lord wants us to use our God-given abilities to find ways to marshal the resources he has placed at our bidding to use and develop them to make an honest living. God's good pleasure and will for us is to *flourish*! So far from being stingy, God has instead given us everything necessary for living life and growing in godly character (2 Peter 1:3). Now to the other part of this little teaching in Matthew 6.

Don't worry! Jesus does not want us to be filled with anxiety over not having what we need. He says the Gentiles (unbelievers) have no faith in the true God, and so they have reason to be filled with anxiety, but not us. In verse 33 he encourages us to "seek first [the Lord's] kingdom and his righteousness, and all these things will be given to you as well." What things? The physical necessities of life! Now we need to be careful here how we take this. He is not saying that we just need to "name it and claim it." He is also not saying, "Give your whole life to God and go live in a monastery, and you will have your needs met." The passage has been interpreted in both those ways, but those interpretations miss the point. What he is saying is that if we seek to be a *kingdom type of people*, then our needs will be met. How so? Well, in part kingdom people are people who follow God's priorities in all of life. They will heed Paul's injunction that if a man does not take care of the basic physical needs of his family, that he is worse than an "infidel" or a person who has no faith (1 Tim. 5:8). A kingdom person will pay heed to the texts we cited in chapter 1 of this book where we discussed the biblical injunction to work. Kingdom kind of people will do those things, and when they do, they will encounter this abundantly wealth-filled world that we live in, and they will find their needs met by God. Most of the time those needs are not met directly (like the bird on the fence with open beak or my hungry, squawking cockatiels), but *indirectly*. Yet they are no less met by the giving God who has given us this world!

Let's round out this discussion by glancing at Jesus' teaching on wealth in his parables. In the parable of the sower (Mark 4:1–20) Jesus taught that the "worries of this world" and the "deceitfulness of riches" can blind a person to the truth of the gospel and insulate a person from the hope of salvation (Mark 4:18). Notice that he did not say that this was inevitable—that rich people can't be saved or that saved people can't be rich—only that it was a danger, a danger that riches might *deceive* us and cause us to hear the Word in an *unfruitful* way. Other parables strike a similar tone. Jesus' parables of the pearl of great price and the treasure in the field (Matt. 13:44–46) juxtapose earthly treasures with heavenly ones and call on us to have the right priorities. The parable of the landowner and the vineyard (Matt. 20:1–13) implies that a contract freely entered into cannot be used to charge an employer (or the Lord) with injustice simply because the outcomes appear to be disparate. Disparate outcomes are simply part of life. I have good friends who make a lot more money than I do, but I do not think that somehow they ought to give some of theirs to me because I am a pastor or just a good guy. Such disparity is simply a fact of life and the way life is.

Jesus also made it clear that those who have the goods of the world need to be generous to those who are lacking. This is part of the lesson of the Good Samaritan (Luke 10:25–37), though that parable certainly has a richer lesson than merely the monetary one. It is incumbent on us to give a cup of water to the "least" of the needy "brothers" we encounter in the course of life in demonstration of the reality of our salvation (Matt. 25:31–46). If we have been guilty of economic deprivation towards others, it is necessary to make restitution (Luke 19:1–10). In each case the object lesson is not so much the benefit that accrues to the poor, but the eternal consequences of being a disciple of Jesus who follows the teaching of his Lord. Kingdom people follow *him*. "The poor you have with you always," Jesus taught (John 12:8 NKJV) as people were rebuking the woman who was lavishing her expensive perfume on him before his arrest. "Let her alone," Jesus ordered them. This woman had her heart right in her attitude toward the Savior, and that was what mattered. There is much more that could be said, but let us now turn to just a smattering of other New Testament texts.

The apostle Paul has many things to say about the handling of wealth. We have noted in the previous chapter that Paul often worked with his hands so as not to be a burden on the people he was serving, but there are several examples of people from other churches sending him financial gifts (see, for example, Phil. 4:16; 2 Cor. 11:9). He also wrote that he had learned to be content with whatever condition he was in, and the context makes it clear that he means his *financial* condition, among other things (Phil. 4:11). He penned words to the Corinthians that when they celebrate the Lord's Supper, that there should be no social class or financial status divisions among them (1 Cor. 11:17–34), since that belies the unity of the body of Christ.

What about giving our wealth away? In 2 Corinthians 8–9, Paul gives specific instructions about giving to others and showing generosity. He uses the Macedonian churches as an example (2 Cor. 8:1–5) and appeals to the ultimate example of Jesus as the guide for living, who "though he was rich, yet for your sakes he became poor, so that you through his poverty might become rich" (8:9). Paul also indicates that he is sending an offering to Corinthians in the hand of Titus so that they might be blessed (8:16–21). He tells them that those who sow sparingly will reap sparingly, but those who sow generously will reap a generous reward, though it is clear from the context that not all such "reaping" will be financial but will often be a reaping of greater opportunities for *service* (2 Cor. 9:6–15). In Romans 15:23–29, Paul mentions an offering for "the poor of . . . Jerusalem" that has been collected by the churches in Macedonia and Achaia, and he urges the Christians in Rome to give generously as well.

One final word from Paul. In a much-cited text, Paul wrote to Timothy, "For the love of money is a root of all sorts of evil" (1 Tim. 6:10 NASB). This passage has been much abused. He does not say that *money* is the root of evil. He does not even say that the love of money is *the* root of *all* evil. He says that the *love* of money is *a* root of all *sorts* of evil. This is not an anti-money verse, but an *anti-misuse* of money text, like much of what we have already seen from Jesus and other biblical teachers.

Few parts in the New Testament have as much to say in such a short span about money and wealth as the letter of James. James writes that genuine religion is a religion that concerns itself with "orphans and widows" (James 1:27). He goes on to say that churches should not show favoritism to the wealthy but should treat rich and poor alike (2:1–7). Those who violate this injunction become "judges with evil thoughts."

He further challenges them not to covet those things that they do not have (James 4:1–3). He says to them that this greed has even infiltrated their prayer life, for they ask and do not receive because they ask with the "wrong motives," that is, that they wish to spend what they get on their "pleasures." This attitude, he writes, constitutes "friendship with the world" and that in essence is "hatred toward God" (v. 4). They leave God out of their approach to life when they say to themselves, "We will go to this or that city, spend a year there, carry on business and make money" (v. 13). He tells them that they should rather say, "If it is the Lord's will, we will live and do this or that" (v. 15).

James addresses the "rich people" of the congregation and tells them that their wealth has rotted and that moths have eaten their clothes, that their gold and silver are corroded. Hear these strong words, "You have hoarded wealth in the last days. Look! The wages you failed to pay to your workmen who mowed your fields are crying out against you" (James 5:3–4). God has heard those cries and condemns the rich for their injustice. To fail to pay an agreed wage is as bad as lust and murder in this passage (v. 6). Strong words, indeed, and it is clear from the text that James is not writing in generalities but knows specifically that these are sins the recipients of his words *have committed*. He calls on them to repent and make restitution.

As the New Testament comes to an end, we find the world in *concerted rebellion* against God, following an evil power (the beast), hoarding its wealth, and making "war against the saints" (Rev. 13:7). Just before the overthrow of this "evil empire" we read that "the kings of the earth committed adultery with her [Babylon], and the merchants of the earth grew rich from her excessive luxuries" (18:3). Now the great city, representing the political and economic systems of the world in rebellion against God, is about to be destroyed by the coming of Christ. "The merchants of the world will weep and mourn over her because no one buys from them anymore. No one buys their gold, silver, jewels, expensive cloth, things made of ivory, bronze, wood, cargoes of spices, of wine and olive oil, of various kinds of food" (vv. 11–13, paraphrase). The great city is about to be thrown down by the returning King of Kings, this place where the merchants were "the world's great men" (v. 23). The *city* of Babylon is being thrown down because in her was found the blood of the prophets and saints, killed because they prophesied against the great political/economic system that had existed since Cain first murdered his own brother all the way back at the other end of the Bible, and then went out and built— a city (Gen. 4:17).

This survey has been necessarily brief. But it at least gives us some idea of what Scripture says about wealth, money, financial obligations, and generosity. As the church has marched its way through history, key teachers have also offered commentary on wealth, and we will skip our way along and look at the most important contributions they have made to this subject.

Understanding the Role of Wealth in Church History

Teachers in the church have held varying views about wealth all through history, in part because they have had to deal with a variety of contexts, both among friends and enemies. In the previous chapter we talked about monasticism and its conviction that the truly spiritual person renounces all worldly goods. That is an extreme position, but others have also gone nearly that far in their criticism of wealth. In the early third century in Carthage, Tertullian was a prominent Christian teacher whose writings have survived to our time. He was an advocate of rigorous holiness in every area of life, including the area of possessions. No monastic, Tertullian believed that Christians had to till the soil, sail in ships, and go to the market with unbelievers. But they should hold wealth in *contempt*. This African church father believed that churches should hold communal purses and simply dole out funds to those who needed to pay bills or purchase food; he further believed that individual Christians should not control their own money. In his words, "Christians have all things in common except wives." This was in effect a kind of churchly socialism.

Another North African church father held a differing position. Born in 354 in Thagaste (modern Algeria), Aurelius Augustine was a precocious child who at age sixteen rejected his mother's Christianity and became a Manichean (an early Christian "cult"). He became a professor of rhetoric, and at the age of thirty-two he was converted to the Christian faith through the influence of his mother, the Bishop of Milan (Ambrose), and the New Testament. He became, in succession, a monk and then the Bishop of Hippo in North Africa, not far from his childhood home. His contributions were enormous, and in the area of a theology of wealth focused on possessions, he made important strides forward. Though he had served as a monk, Augustine rejected the *extreme* forms of asceticism (self-denial) that had become common among some monastics. He knew that people can be too *acquisitive* in regard to possessions, but he also believed that there was a role for *commerce* and that wickedness was not necessarily inherent in commercial activity. He also argued that profit in business was acceptable in the Christian worldview. As Rodney Stark has noted, "In this way, Augustine gave legitimacy not merely to merchants but to the eventual deep involvement of the church in the birth of capitalism."

Augustine made three contributions to a Christian theology of possessions. First, he distinguished between material things and the *possession* of those things. Since God is Creator, material things themselves are intrinsically good, a point we have made earlier in this chapter. Second, Augustine made a distinction between using material possessions, and *enjoying* them. In his book *On Christian Doctrine*, Augustine stated, "Some things are to be enjoyed, others are to be used, and there are others to be enjoyed and used." Think of a house. A house provides basic shelter, a place to raise a family, a place to offer hospitality. We can even be grateful for the fact that we own a *nice* home, but there is always the danger of excessive *pride* or even idolatry in that. Third, the best thing that one can do with possessions is to *give* them away. But there is no outside constraint when it comes to generosity. It is perfectly fine to have possessions, but one should also be willing to relinquish them when one becomes aware of a need that one can meet. This is neither churchly confiscation nor governmental confiscation; it is a freewill gift in Augustine's view.

It should be obvious that Augustine represents a very different approach than that of the monks or of Tertullian, though *not* a completely opposite approach. All of these were in a process of trying to integrate biblical teaching with a contemporary situation, but there is clearly a kind of rational utility factor to Augustine's approach to the Bible not found in the others we have discussed so far. Augustine in some ways was the founder of what we might call "rational theology," the application of reason and an understanding of natural law to the interpretation and application of Scripture.

Here we will leap forward to the thirteenth century to the next major contributor to our theology of wealth and finances. In the 1220s a group of Arab, Jewish, and Christian scholars collaborated in the city of Toledo, Spain, to translate the works of Aristotle into Latin, the common language of educated Western Europe. (Arabic translations from the Greek had already been made.) Aristotle had written in the fourth century BC on topics such as logic, metaphysics (the nature of existence), epistemology (how we know what we know), and other important intellectual matters, but his works had been lost to the Latin speaking West and had been relegated to the dust pile even in his native land. This rediscovery sent shock waves through the intellectual world of Catholic Christianity and sparked a revitalization of scholarly theology and science that would transform the Western world. This set the stage for the rise of new theological discourses and methods, new explorations in philosophy, and within three centuries the rise of modern natural science.

The most outstanding representative of this new intellectual climate was Thomas Aquinas. Born to a noble and wealthy family, Thomas had several older brothers who would inherit the family fortune, but Thomas would be relegated to a Benedictine monastery, with the family's expectation that he would, through natural gifts and patronage from his father, rise to become abbot of one of the great monasteries. Thomas, to his family's chagrin, elected to become a *Dominican* monk, one of the "new orders" that had arisen shortly before his birth. In his family's view, this would prevent him from a prestigious career. To the contrary, he achieved renown and distinction as a scholar and wrote several great books, laying the foundations for modern Catholic thought. In the area of economic theory he would be the scholar who would also lay the foundations for modern economics, a topic we will return to in a later chapter. Here I merely wish to outline his theological beliefs about wealth and its use by Christians.

Thomas, following Aristotle, founded his views on the use of wealth on *natural-law theory*, which he also combined with the teachings of Scripture and the church. Natural law teaches us that humans have a right to proprietorship over goods—the right to private property. Private ownership of property was necessary due to human sin. If something belongs to everyone, no one takes care of it. If ownership is valid, then anything that infringes on private ownership is itself a sin. So larceny and pillaging are wrong. His second principle was that although private property claims are valid, the use of all things should be available to *all* who have need. So those who are rich in the world's goods should share freely with those in need, seeing that as a God-given mandate. Further, if the poor man is in urgent and manifest need (his family is starving, for instance), he is justified in taking what he needs to satisfy in a temporary sense that urgent and manifest need, even to the point of trickery or violence. The state has no authority in these matters, but church, culture, and society have to find a way to work these things out.

Though ahead of the curve in understanding economics, in commerce and trade issues Thomas was a man of his times. Contrary to Augustine, who was quite foresighted, Thomas did not believe in the moral acceptability of profits derived from commerce. He contended for a barter system with no profit motive. Further, he urged that loans be given with no interest built in. Making a profit, whether in business or in loaning money, was *selfish* and violated

God's law in Thomas's thinking. But a more sober and reasoned understanding of these important matters was on the horizon.

We have already discussed John Calvin's views on work and vocation. He also made important contributions to a theology of wealth. Wealth in and of itself, for Calvin, is neither moral nor immoral. In a recent biography, Bruce Gordon wrote, "[Calvin] was not opposed to the market per se and even became involved in financial transactions by recommending speculative investments to friends and by securing loans for recently arrived immigrants." Calvin also rejected the medieval Catholic injunction against charging interest on loans. Thomas Aquinas and other Catholic thinkers, as we saw, believed that charging interest violated the Old Testament teaching on the sin of usury, and Martin Luther, Calvin's German contemporary, agreed with that. (Someone has said that Luther was actually a man of the fifteenth century on the theology of wealth, while Calvin was a man of the seventeenth century. Of course, they both lived in the sixteenth century.) Calvin recognized that lenders took a *risk* in loaning money, and that, since borrowers are sinners, some of them would not pay back the loans. He argued that usury actually happens when someone charges *too much* interest. He led the pastors of the city of Geneva to ban from the Lord's Supper any lender who charged more than 5 percent interest, but as long as the interest did not exceed that, it was in line with what Calvin called "biblical realism." These and other reforms in business, banking, and other areas of the economy resulted in Geneva becoming one of the most thriving cities in Europe by the time Calvin died in 1564.

Conclusion

We could certainly say more about the theology of wealth and finance, but the basic biblical and theological contours have been sketched out in this chapter. God is the maker of wealth. In a fallen world, Christian believers have to live disciplined and circumspect lives to ensure that they are using the wealth God has given to them in ways that honor him. Having personal possessions and property is a good thing, and much good can accrue from their usage. Differences in social standing based on property ought not to be extended to our church life, where all are equal before the Lord. Those who have little in the way of the world's goods should nonetheless work hard and honor God with what little they have. Those who have been blessed with an abundance (rich and poor alike) should be very concerned to be generous with those in need, and generous to extend the Lord's work to the ends of the earth through their diverse callings and the wealth they produce to extend the gospel and Christ's kingdom.

Study Questions

1. Do you believe that monasticism and Tertullian best represent the teachings of Jesus on money and wealth, or do you think Augustine and Calvin had a more biblical view?

2. Using the Scripture texts cited early on in this chapter, do you think that the Bible overall has a positive or a negative view on wealth and its accumulation?

3. Based on the materials presented here and from your own experience, what are some ways churches can help those who are in financial need?

4. In the section above where we discussed Thomas Aquinas, we noted that he believed that making a profit was a sin. From the Bible texts we discussed, do you agree or disagree with him? Why?

5. Calvin, Thomas Aquinas, and Augustine all presented what we called here a "rational theology" that led to certain conclusions both in theological doctrine and in areas such as politics and economics. What do you think of this idea of rational theology?

For Further Reading

Brand, Chad, and Tom Pratt. *Seeking the City: Christian Faith and Political Economy; A Biblical, Theological, Historical Study.* Grand Rapids: Kregel, 2013.

Gordon, Bruce. *Calvin.* New Haven: Yale University Press, 2009.

Mueller, John. *Redeeming Economics: Discovering the Missing Element.* Wilmington, DE: ISI Books, 2010.

Stark, Rodney. *The Victory of Reason: How Christianity Led to Freedom, Capitalism, and Western Success.* New York: Random House, 2005.

Wheatley, Alan B. *Patronage in Early Christianity: Its Use and Transformation from Jesus to Paul of Samosata.* Eugene, OR: Wipf and Stock / Pickwick Publications, 2011.

The City of Man | 4

Before the fall of Adam, the institution of government was not necessary. God was ruler and Adam was his viceroy. Politics was not even a prospective topic. After the fall, however, government and politics became necessary. The church father Augustine in his famous book, *City of God*, made this very point. Had there been no sin, there would never have been a political state, for, though man is naturally *sociable*, he is not naturally *political*. That book by the African church father explained that there are two cities in the world: the City of God and the City of Man. The City of God depicts the rule of God in the hearts of those who love him, while the City of Man depicts that company of men and women who are dominated by self-love rather than by love for God. This distinction is exemplified in the world of human governments. It is possible for those who are part of the City of God to be rulers of human governments; in fact, that would be preferable. But in Augustine's view that was not the case with Rome, nor is it often the case anywhere.

In the previous three chapters, we have first developed a theology of work and then a theology of wealth. What we will examine and attempt to do in this chapter is to sketch the contours of a theology of politics, or a *political theology*.

The City of Man in the Old Testament

The first attempt on the part of one man to rule over other men was Cain, who, rather than "mastering" his sin (Gen. 4:7), mastered his brother and took his brother's life. He then went out and built a city that he named after his son Enoch (Gen. 4:17). This city of Enoch, like the one that is depicted in Genesis 11 (Babel), would become a place where those who are dominated by self-love will flee both to find a sense of anonymity and a place of distorted fellowship with others who do not love God. Other cities followed suit, and so Sodom and Gomorrah (Gen. 19) stand out in the early pages of the Bible as places of dark wickedness that call forth the judgmental hand of the Lord in their destruction.

The story is not all one of darkness and gloom, though, when it comes to human government. When Joseph rises to a high position of leadership in Egypt in the later chapters of Genesis, the administration of the Egyptian pharaoh is benevolent toward his own people, and even toward the family of Joseph, who "migrate" to Egypt during the years of the famine that comes upon the land (see Gen. 37–50). Then, after the exodus from Egypt some four hundred years after the time of Joseph, and after Israel had conquered the land of Canaan, and after about another four hundred years had elapsed, the people of Israel begged their judge and prophet Samuel to anoint them a king. The people had become weary of the cycle of defeat and rescue followed again and again by defeat and rescue, which was characteristic of the period of the judges depicted especially in the book by that name and also in the early chapters of 1 Samuel. The Israelites longed for a king, "like all the other nations," to give them security against the warring nations around them (1 Sam. 8). God had promised that he would fight for them as long as they were faithful to the covenant (Deut. 28). But consistent covenant faithfulness proved to be a hard task for Israel to maintain. If they had a king to consolidate their tribes and to give them a central governing authority, perhaps the occasional slip into spiritual failure would not be so catastrophic.

In 1 Samuel 8 we find God's fascinating response to their request, issued through the prophet Samuel. First, God tells Samuel that this desire for a king is a tacit rejection of the kinghood of the Lord, and he reminds Samuel that they have repeatedly rejected God's rule in their nation over the previous four centuries by their recurring resort to "other gods" (vv. 6–8). But then, somewhat surprisingly, he grants their insolent request. Not, however, before divulging to the people the implications of having an earthly king, implications that include high taxation, military and political conscription, and other infringements on what had previously been their own livelihoods and freedoms (vv. 9–20). One lesson to learn from this text is that this is the way it will be with centralized governments. And the more centralized and powerful, the more the prerogatives and freedom of the people will be diminished.

Samuel seeks out and anoints Saul to be the first king of Israel. Outwardly, this seems to be a good choice. Saul is tall and from a respected family in Israel, and he is a dutiful son and apparently humble, all good qualities in one who would be king of Israel (1 Sam. 9). He looked "kingly" (or as we would say, "he looks presidential"). But for those of us who have read the rest of the story, we know that things turned out quite differently. King Saul in time showed himself to be a man unable to control his emotions, incapable of sustaining genuine loyalty to God, and unable really to command the love and affection of his people. He became jealous of others, including his own son, and became murderous.

He defied the explicit commands of the prophet Samuel, and at the end of the day he died by his own hand (1 Sam. 31).

God, however, has another plan, and that plan is named David. In many ways, David appears to be the "anti-Saul." He does not cut an imposing figure. God speaks to the prophet and tells him that outward appearance is not the criterion for service, but rather, the inward heart (1 Sam. 16:7). God wants a man to be king who has a heart for the Lord. In the narrative that stretches from 1 Samuel 16 to 2 Samuel 10, David seems clearly to be that man. Not that all of his decisions or actions are free from foolishness or sin. In his rash anger at one point he comes close to murder (1 Sam. 25). He later lies to a Philistine king (1 Sam. 27–29). He is guilty of excessive bloodshed on several occasions, with the result that the Lord tells David that he will not build a temple to the Lord, but rather his son Solomon will (2 Sam. 7:5–16). Later, he fails at bringing discipline into his own household, with the later result of military rebellion and revolution on the part of his son Absalom (2 Sam. 13–18).

David is an imperfect man, but his commendable qualities are still quite apparent. His own people loved him; he did not supplant Saul and take the kingship for himself even though he had already been anointed and had several "circumstantial" opportunities to do so; he waited on God to bring his deliverances, even when this waiting lasted years; he loved the Lord with all his heart, in spite of his foolish choices and sins; when he was confronted with his sin, he made no excuses but poured out his soul, not only in private to God but publicly in the form of psalms of confession that he penned (Pss. 32; 51). In virtually all of these examples, he shows himself to be the great contrast to his predecessor, Saul. David's government is not perfect, but it sets a pattern for godly governing that is unrivaled in the sinful and politically corrupt world of the Old Testament, establishing the kind of precedent that results in God promising that the scepter would never depart from David's house and that his kingdom would be an eternal one (2 Sam. 7:16; Pss. 2; 45).

At the death of David, his son Solomon became king in his place. Solomon, unlike his father, had grown up in as much luxury as was available to a tenth-century-BC Israelite. He had watched his father lead a powerful administrative state that had been successful in war and that had come to control virtually all of its nearby national competitors. He had also observed as his father put down an insurrection from within his own family. He understood power, or at least he thought he did, and when he came to the throne he was committed to maintaining a strong governmental hand, even one stronger than that of David.

His father, on his deathbed, instructed Solomon to deal harshly with most of the ones who had either deeply disappointed David or who represented threats to the security of Solomon once he became king. In a manner similar to the ending of a *Godfather* film, he had his half-brother Adonijah killed, he exiled the priest Abiathar, he had the former general of David's army, Joab, assassinated, and eventually had Shimei, a man who had cursed David when he was deposed and then repented when he returned, killed as well (all of this is related in 1 Kings 2). Then Solomon in prayer to God asked for wisdom to govern wisely, and there are several examples of this remarkable wisdom recorded in the biblical narrative (1 Kings 3–4). But embedded in the story are signs of trouble to come.

Solomon accumulated great wealth due to heavy taxation, wealth that included imported weapons and horses (2 Chron. 1:14–17) and imported wood and other building materials to be used in the construction of the temple, but also in the construction of a very ornate kingly palace (2 Chron. 2–7; 1 Kings 7). The utensils for the temple were also very expensive (2 Chron. 4). The reputation of his wealth spread far and wide so that when dignitaries, like the Queen of Sheba, visited, they testified both to his great wisdom and wealth, and added more wealth besides, the queen herself giving Solomon 120 talents of gold, an amount equal to around nine thousand pounds of gold! (A solid cube of gold 14.2 inches on each side weighs one ton. The African queen basically brought Solomon the equivalent of four and a half of these.) That is a lot of gold! One has to wonder what intentions lay behind such a gift!

That gold had to come from somewhere. If it was brought by the Queen of Sheba, and the text says that it was, she must in some manner have *extracted* it from her own people or from nations with which she had gone to war. The gold came from somewhere; it did not just appear out of thin air as an answer to prayer. A further account of the extent of Solomon's great wealth can be found in 2 Chronicles 9:13–28, and the list is *staggering*. You have to remember as you read this, that this is treasure flowing into governmental coffers. Solomon did not create or *produce* wealth; he extracted it. Though little is actually said in the first nine chapters of 2 Chronicles that reflects negatively on Solomon's wealth, any sensitive reader will have been alerted to these economic and political issues, and then in chapter 10 the criticism becomes explicit.

If Solomon was born with a silver spoon in his mouth, his son Rehoboam was born with a golden one in his. As the son took the throne at the death of his father, he consulted with his father's "cabinet." The people had already spoken to Rehoboam and informed him that Solomon had "put a heavy yoke" on them, a yoke of a heavy-handed, centralized government exercising its will in an unimpeded manner. Solomon had been a tax-and-spend guy. "How would you advise me to answer these people?" That was Rehoboam's question to the elders. Their immediate response makes it clear that Solomon's fiscal policies had been nothing short of *confiscation*, confiscation for the glory of his own kingdom. (After all, no king wants to be ruler over a poor and puny state!) His father's advisors replied, "Be kind to these people and please them and give them a favorable answer." In other words, "Cut taxes! Give us smaller government! Stop intruding on our freedoms!" At least they said it in a *kind* manner (all this is related in 2 Chron. 10:1–7).

Rehoboam, however, chose to listen instead to advice from his younger peers, young men of court who had also grown up in luxury and prestige. Their advice: "Tell the people who have asked you to lighten the load that the load is about to get much heavier. Tell them that your father scourged them with whips, but you will scourge them with scorpions" (2 Chron. 10:8–11, paraphrase). In other words, government is about to get even bigger, and the people will simply have to put up with it. If you know the rest of the story, you know they did *not* put up with it. Ten of the twelve tribes of the nation of Israel (the northern-most tribes) seceded from the union and went to war to secure that secession.

Gone were the "days of wine and roses" that had characterized the rule of David, and especially of Solomon. Solomon had pushed the size of government too far, and now the governments of both nations, Israel and Judah, would shrink back due to a variety of factors, not least of which was the unwillingness of the people to finance such an uncontrollable and spendthrift system. Gone also, for the most part, were the days of the kings ruling as viceroys for the Lord. David was a man after God's heart, with some significant failures, but still God's man; Solomon began well, though ended with idolatry in his own household and an inability, for one so wise, to control his need for women—*lots* of women. And he built a giant administrative state that brought him fame and glory. But from this point on, the northern nation of Israel would have no godly kings, and the southern nation of Judah would have only a few. The rule of God over the house of David would go into eclipse, appearing a few more brief times before conquest and exile would remove the people, temporarily at least, from their inheritance. God's people would have to wait more centuries before the true Son of David would make his appearance in a manger in David's ancestral home of Bethlehem. But what else does Scripture teach us about the City of Man?

One thing it teaches is that God's people must be loyal to the Lord, even if it brings them into *conflict* with the state. When the nation of Judah was conquered by King Nebuchadnezzar of Babylon in 604 BC, many of its citizens, especially young men from noble houses, were carried off to Babylon for repatriation as loyal citizens of the new power. The Babylonians reasoned that if these young Israelites were raised as young Babylonians, there would be little likelihood that they would one day seek revenge in some kind of retaliatory war against Babylon. Four of those young men, however, resisted being "Babylonianized," and made a commitment to be faithful to the God of their fathers, even though most of their immediate fathers had not been so faithful. Under intense pressure to conform to the new order, they decided to retain their commitment to the dietary laws given by Moses, to keep the words of the Ten Commandments, to resist any attempts to force them to bow to foreign gods, and to remain faithful to pray to and maintain personal devotion to the God of Israel. This, in spite of persecution, and even in the face of almost certain death (see Dan. 1–4).

Sometimes the question is raised, "What does the Bible teach us about submitting to governing powers?" The lesson from Daniel, repeated in other places, is that we submit to governing powers unless they call on us to do that which violates our primary commitment to be faithful to God and his Word. If we have to choose, we decide to follow the Lord, despite the consequences, even death. There is a broader question, which might be stated like this: What is a biblical theology of governance or of politics? Of course, if we try to find such an answer in the Bible, we always have to consider the biblical and historical context of the passages we are looking at. Is the ruler in this passage of the Bible King David or King Nebuchadnezzar? Is the ruler one who is attempting to serve the Lord, as even Nebuchadnezzar did at some points in the book of Daniel (or as Pharaoh did during the days of Joseph)? Or is the ruler, like King Ahab of Israel, a vile and wicked man who seeks only his own benefit, even though he is king of Israel? Any theology of politics may proceed in interpreting what the Bible says about such a thing only if we note what is going on historically, culturally, and morally in the context of the event or passage.

The City of Man in the New Testament

What about the City of Man in the New Testament? The New Testament offers not quite the same wealth of information as we find in the Old Testament, but several passages will both confirm our Old Testament observations and advance the discussion to some extent.

We discussed in chapter 1 that Jesus was born into a world of political patronage. Rome forced its will on its provinces, which included Judea and Galilee, ruthlessly and often at sword point. This was no "benevolent empire," but a top-heavy, tax-heavy administrative state that curbed any attempt at rebellion quickly and efficiently. Judean farmers, like those in much of Rome's empire, turned over one-third of their crop to the Roman government. There were other taxes, such as the temple tax, so that many even of the poor people were doling out nearly half of their meager earnings to the state.

Yet Jesus did not come preaching revolution or even political reformation, but instead he told his disciples to "render to Caesar the things that are Caesar's; and to God the things that are God's" (Matt. 22:21 NASB). In some ways this statement by Jesus represents the *foundational text* for both a *political theology* and for real religious liberty. God has ultimate claim over our life; a government's claim is more limited, yet still real. At his own trial Jesus submitted to the governing will of the *junta* that included

Annas, Herod, and Pilate. He made tacit claim to being "the king of the Jews," and Pilate mocked him by hanging a trilingual placard on his cross, cynically demonstrating what he, Pilate, would do to such "kings." Jesus rendered to God that which was his, but also respected the claims of Caesar.

When we come to the book of Acts, we find the apostles in a similar position with regard to the state as Jesus had been in his arrest and execution. They are called before the Sanhedrin, the ruling council among the Jews in Judaism. The priests and others who formed that group commanded them no longer to preach in the name of Jesus (Acts 4:18), but Peter and John, representing the others, replied, "Judge for yourselves whether it is right in God's sight to obey you rather than God. For we cannot help speaking about what we have seen and heard" (vv. 19–20). That response may well have recalled to the biblically literate people who heard it the account of the Hebrew teenagers in the book of Daniel.

It did not end there. Stephen, called on the carpet before the same body, reminded them that their own forefathers, political leaders in Israel, had killed the prophets who went before and were those who predicted the coming of the Righteous One (Acts 7:51–53). The council then punctuated his final remarks by stoning him (vv. 54–60). Saul (later renamed Paul) then proceeded to launch a *pogrom* against Christians. James would be the first apostle killed with the sword, Peter imprisoned, and eventually after seeing the risen Lord Jesus on the road to Damascus the now-converted Paul would be arrested in Jerusalem and imprisoned for four years before appearing before the emperor in Rome. And of course, he would also later be "poured out" in a final appearance before imperial authorities and his life taken from him (see his final written words in 2 Timothy).

Paul himself in writing to the church in the city of Rome (the seat of the persecutorial empire) would give his own inspired instructions for how one ought to relate to the governing authorities, whatever and whoever they may be. He instructed them, "Everyone must submit to the governing authorities, for there is no authority that has not been established by God. So, he who rebels against authority is resisting what God has established, and those who do so will bring judgment on themselves. . . . [The governing authority] is God's servant to do you good. . . . Therefore it is necessary to submit to authority, not only because of punishment but also because of conscience" (Rom. 13:1–5, paraphrase). Notice that he uses the word "submit" in verses 1 and 5, rather than the term "obey," perhaps because he knew that, while Christians could submit to their ruling authorities, they would probably not be able to obey them *in every area*. As we have discussed with the Israelites in Babylon and the apostles in Jerusalem, sometimes one must choose between the state and God. Paul notes that there is no authority except that which God has established (v. 1), and that is true even of the authority of Satan as the opening chapters of the book of Job make clear. Everett Harrison in his commentary on this passage notes that the name of Jesus is not found in this paragraph, probably since "the thought does not move in the sphere of redemption or the life of the church, as such, but in the relation to the state that God in his wisdom has set up." I think that is correct.

Those who refuse submission to the state are in rebellion against God. States may make demands that Christians cannot comply with, but *anarchy* is not the antidote to that. One way to think about this text is to see it as "when the state is functioning in the way that it should." The role of government is to provide security for its citizens from dangerous threats both within and from without, to provide stability to commercial transactions, ease of travel from one part of the country to another, insofar as possible to create the conditions conducive to economic stability, and beyond that to give people as much freedom to live their lives in the way they see fit. Paul may be envisioning something like this in his idealization of the state, especially in verses 3 and 4. Of course, neither in Rome then nor in many other places since has such an idealized state been the case. In those situations, as German scholar Ernst Käsemann has put it, "Sometimes the Lord of the world speaks more audibly out of prison cells and graves than out of the life of the churches which congratulate themselves on their concordat with the State." Discipleship sometimes puts us in conflict with the state, and then we must choose: *Kaiser Kurios* or *Christos Kurios*? In the words of Martin Niemöller of Germany in the 1930s, "Gott ist mein Führer!"

As we noted in chapter 3 on wealth, the book of Revelation shows us the escalation of a world in rebellion as the coming of Christ draws near. It is, as we showed, an economic coalition in rebellion against God, yet it is also a *political* conspiracy under the ultimate direction of Satan, and also under the penultimate direction of the Beast of Revelation (Rev. 13), whom Paul called "the man of lawlessness" (2 Thess. 2:1–10), whom Jesus called "the abomination of desolation" (Matt. 24:15), and whom John referred to as "the antichrist" (1 John 4:3). It is as though all of the despots of history were to coalesce into one man and one system of terrorism and totalitarianism. What is depicted is a final statist attempt to control all wealth, all weapons, all governments, and all the people and to unite in one great last-ditch effort to dethrone God. But it is an effort that will fail, and after Jesus destroys his enemies, then he will hand over "the kingdom to God the Father after he has destroyed all dominion, authority and power" (1 Cor. 15:24). Then God will truly be King!

Church and State in History: A Political Theology?

From the earliest days of Christianity the church has had to find a way to dwell within the City of Man. We can only touch on a few samplings of this endeavor in the space that we have. We have already seen how early Christianity squared off against the Jewish Sanhedrin and against the Roman Empire. In the third century the Roman emperors Decius (249–51), Valerian (258–60), and Diocletian (303–11) launched three different imperial persecutions that cost thousands of lives and killed (or severely injured) key church bishops and leaders, especially men like Cyprian of Carthage and Origen of Alexandria. But in 313 Constantine authorized the Edict of Milan, ending the persecutions, essentially for good. Later that century when Emperor Theodosius, as we mentioned in chapter 2, made Christianity the official religion of the empire, to many people it seemed that a kind of millennial kingdom had arrived. However, this created a symbiosis between church and state that in many ways was more damaging to genuine Christianity than the persecutions had been. When Christianity is the state church of a governing power, and in some sense under that governing power's directive, every aberration imaginable can be cooked up by one side or the other and presented as the "True Faith." *Christendom* had arrived! But how *Christian* was Christendom?

Augustine was watching those very things happening when he penned his famous book, *City of God*. He did hope for a day when the City of Man and the City of God would become nearly unified. (He realized that the true City of God in all its glory would not come until Christ fulfilled all things.) One mighty king in the eighth and ninth centuries who believed that he might just be the man to unite the two cities was Charlemagne.

Charles the Great inherited the Kingdom of the Franks from his father, Pippin the Short, in 768. On Christmas Day, AD 800, Pope Leo III crowned him "Emperor of the Romans," thus restoring the Western Roman Empire that had fallen to the barbarians in 476. The Eastern Roman Empire (what we now generally call the Byzantine Empire) had remained intact, and would continue until its fall at the hands of the Turks in 1453. But the Pope needed a

Western ally and Charles needed papal recognition. Charlemagne was at the same time a very devout man in his faith and a very fierce and violent enemy to the Saxons and others who stood in the way of his vision for Christian imperialism. One of his favorite books (he could read, but not write well) was Augustine's *City of God*. One can imagine him, sitting near a fire under the stars in one of his campaigns against the Saxons, listening to one of his priests reading from the famous tome, fingering his sword hilt and muttering under his breath, "And God will use me to make it happen." The "marriage" brought about between church and state by the papal coronation cemented in a more powerful way than ever the close ties between these two entities; yet the centuries that lay ahead would prove this to be a shaky marriage, indeed!

We have previously made mention of Thomas Aquinas in reference to a theology of wealth and finance. He also made important contributions to *political theology*, and gave what Mark Lilla has called "the most coherent account of Christian political life" up to that time. Thomas argued that the incarnation of Christ makes the possibility of a truly Christian state with a truly Christian monarch a real possibility. Borrowing from Aristotle, Thomas contended that humans are political animals (that is, they are living beings operating in a *polis*, a city) and that political life can help human society to move closer to perfection. Recall that Augustine was not so optimistic about this because of the nature of human sin. Thomas accepted Augustine's views on original sin, but he also believed that Aristotle had been on to something, and that is likely why this otherwise Augustinian thinker had a higher assessment of the possibilities for Christian monarchy than did Augustine.

John Calvin also weighed in on the arena of *political theology*. Civil government is a force for good, for Calvin, and is the instrument that keeps men from descending into chaos. If it were not for civil government, men would do whatever they pleased, since, as he put it in the *Institutes*, they would go "scot-free." Government does not have a merely negative role but a positive one as well. Again, in the *Institutes*, he wrote that government was "to cherish and protect the outward worship of God, to defend sound doctrine of piety and the position of the church, to adjust our life to the society of men, to form our social behavior to civil righteousness, to reconcile us with one another, and to promote general peace and tranquility." In other words, godly magistrates could provide biblical and rational leadership and work with godly pastors to govern both church and state in a manner that would please God. Civil government does more than bear the sword, though it certainly does that; it is also our teacher and mentor.

Calvin held the same view of human depravity as the previous two thinkers (Augustine and Thomas), but his understanding of how governance works differed from both of them. Contrary to Thomas, he was *not* convinced that rule by a godly king was possible, but (contrary to Augustine) he did believe in the possibility of a Christian *state*. Calvin did not believe that Scripture gave a specific prescription for a certain kind of government or that only one kind of government would work. But he believed that to place all authority in the hands of one person or only a handful of elites was unwise. When he lectured on Amos 7 he blasted the governments of Germany and England and referred to Henry VIII as a "blasphemy." Calvin believed that some blend of aristocracy and democracy would be best; not an aristocracy of hereditary right, but a class of leaders elected by their fellows. He favored the idea of decentralization in politics. Herbert Foster has argued that Calvin held to five principles in political theory: "fundamental law, natural rights, contract and consent of [the] people, popular sovereignty, [and] resistance to tyranny through responsible representatives," what Foster calls the "five points of political Calvinism." This is an advance over previous discussions, an advance made not by a philosopher but by a pastor.

The Genevan Reformer was opposed to rebellion and revolution. He contended that if a people have an oppressive monarch, that it might be, as in the case with Nebuchadnezzar in the Old Testament, God's way of disciplining them for their sin. Israel did not rise in revolution against the Babylonians and neither should we when we are in such straits. Calvin did, however, believe that there might come some situations where lesser magistrates might come together to remove an oppressive ruler, and that if they do not do so, they "fraudulently betray the liberty of the people" over which they have been placed as guardians. Much more could be said, but this outline of the main features of Calvin's political theology gives us the general contours of his thought.

As helpful and innovative as Calvin's vision was, it was also flawed in the minds of some on one point. His exposition necessarily entailed that the church would in some manner be under the tutelage or mandate of the state, and the same can be said of the model begun several years prior to Calvin's efforts in the Swiss city of Zurich. But a protest movement in that city soon set in. On January 21, 1525, a small group of men gathered at the home of one Felix Manz. For two years prior the city council of Zurich had been working toward the same kind of reforms that Luther had established in Saxony (this work in Zurich was eleven years earlier than the work of Calvin). They had hired a former priest and prominent scholar named Ulrich Zwingli to lead the reform efforts. The men who gathered in Manz's home were students of Zwingli's at the university in Zurich, but this group had come to a point of disagreement with their professor. They could find no evidence in the New Testament for infant baptism, but only for believer's baptism, or, more specifically, for *disciple's baptism*. This entailed for them also a new view of the church, that it was a *believer's church*. This brought them into conflict with both the ancient Roman Catholic tradition and the newer Reformation churches that were forming (Lutheran and Reformed at the time, and later, Anglican).

A later convert to this view, former priest Menno Simons, believed that these "Anabaptists" (a term that means re-baptizers) were simply applying Luther's doctrine of justification by faith to their understanding of the church. He believed that they were completing the Reformation begun by Luther by taking it to its logical conclusion—that if one is justified by a *volitional* decision of faith, that one's membership in the local church should also be a result of one's *conscious choice*, and not by a decision of one's family or by edict of the government.

The age-old practice of infant baptism had enormous implications. (It can be traced back to the third century.) As James Payton Jr. has noted, "Social expectations, legal enactments and interpersonal relationships all built on this foundation. So to deny that the paedo-baptism [infant baptism] of all was legitimate and to insist on a later baptism of only a few could not be a personal decision with the goal of pursuing greater spiritual fidelity. It also entailed a stinging indictment of the Christian faith of the others and of the legitimacy of the civil state." In other words, the leaders of Zurich came quickly to view the Anabaptists as *treasonous*. Zurich had a law (and so did most other governments at the time) that demanded that infants be "christened" within thirty days of birth. This made them members of the religio-political order and made them accountable to both church and state. The Radical Reformers (the Anabaptists) were protesting a religious and theological practice, but it was a practice tied to civil obedience as well. They were intent on separating the church from the state in this regard, but the Zurich authorities viewed their practice as sedition, and outlawed re-baptism. Felix Manz was executed by *drowning* in 1527 in parody of their practice.

The Radical Reformers (a term coined by author and professor George Hunston Williams), so called because they believed church reforms should go right to the root (Latin, *radix*), believed that simply altering one's view of salvation or authority was not enough left alone. The other forms of "Reformation"—Lutheran, Reformed, and Anglican—were all either initiated by ruling authorities or somehow overseen by them. The Radicals, though, were convinced that the church should reform *itself*, without government assistance. Their reasoning was that if you get government *assistance* in carrying out needed reforms, you will also get government *interference*, an interference that often has the self-interest of the state at heart. That was in fact exactly what *did happen* in all of the versions of magisterial Reform (so called because it entailed the assistance of magistrates), whether under Zwingli, Calvin, or Thomas Cranmer with Henry VIII in England. Some of the Radicals of course were *extremists*, or "radicals," in the way we usually think of that word, and took control of cities, engaged in armed revolution, and made extravagant claims about the second coming of Christ. Most of them, however, were evangelical in their theology, men, like Menno Simons and Conrad Grebel, who simply wanted to evangelize the masses and carry out their theological and churchly programs without governmental intrusion. They did not believe in the possibility of a Christian state in *this age*. Grebel himself refused to accept the jurisdiction of the town council over his congregation, and paid for it with months in jail. In the words of Mennonite theology professor Harold Bender, this courageous action "planted the seed" out of which has grown the Protestant commitment to "freedom of conscience, freedom of religion, voluntary church membership, and separation of church and state." Pretty important stuff!

Let's leap forward about eighty years to the year 1630. In chapter 2 we discussed the arrival in Massachusetts of the Puritans, who built a sort of paradise there in the wilderness. There are also some things we can learn from them about the development of the City of Man. Their basic philosophy was that there would be two institutions in their society led by two distinct kinds of leaders. The churches were to be governed by godly pastors and elders, while the civil sphere was to be led by godly magistrates. Ideally, these two "offices" would not blur their distinctiveness, but, also ideally, they would work together to ensure a peaceful, orderly, and godly society. Things seldom work out the way you plan, and both "ideals" proved difficult to maintain.

Pastor John Cotton arrived from England in 1633, together with a number of members of his church back in England. A titanic intellect and charismatic individual, Cotton's presence was soon felt all through New England, whose primary towns at this time were Boston and Salem. He preached the twofold covenants of grace and works. God had given the covenant of works to Adam—obey God and all will be well. After Adam sinned God initiated the covenant of grace whereby sinners (all of us) could be saved through Christ. For Cotton, both covenants were still in effect, with the covenant of grace pertaining to our spiritual life and the hope for salvation, and the covenant of works governing our daily relational experiences, including work, family, economics, and politics. Because both of these areas, the spiritual life and the arena of working, exchanging, and governing, were under the watch-care of pastors, sermons sometimes did blur the distinction between church and state.

In addition, Cotton was convinced that the churches in the colony needed to walk lockstep with one another theologically. When a member of his church, Anne Hutchinson, was brought up on heresy charges, he at first defended her. But when the nature of her beliefs finally came out, Hutchinson was banished. Roger Williams, another Puritan who had come from England earlier than Cotton, ran afoul of Cotton's attempt to homogenize New England theology. Williams moved to Rhode Island, where he founded Providence Plantation and became, briefly, a Baptist. Williams then decided that there was no true church in the world since the succession of true churches had long since failed, and, while he continued to evangelize Native Americans, he did not establish "churches." Williams did, however, continue to oppose Cotton's heavy-handed approach to religious enforcement of his ideas.

In 1644 Williams wrote *The Bloudy Tenent of Persecution*, a critique of the Puritans' attempts at forcing theological conformity in Massachusetts. One might think that the Puritans would be strong proponents of religious liberty, since part of the reason they came to America was that they were being persecuted for their beliefs in England. But that was not to be the case. Believing that theological uniformity was necessary to the political stability of Massachusetts, they used the power of the state to enforce their views. To the Puritans, religion was so important that it demanded state support (see Thomas Kidd, *God of Liberty*). For Williams, state support of religion would inevitably mean state support of only one form of religion, and that would rob individuals who were persuaded that another form of religion was correct to sacrifice their natural right to worship in the manner they chose. The debate between Cotton and Williams would continue for years, but by the 1650s Massachusetts had for the most part curtailed its efforts at enforcing theological conformity.

By 1740 the dynamic of Christianity had largely waned from most of the colonies, the exception being Massachusetts, which had been ignited by revivals beginning in 1734. In 1740 an Anglican priest from England began a tour of the colonies (his second one) that would sweep between twenty-five thousand and fifty thousand "Americans" into the kingdom of God. His message was the "new birth," and the need for a personal encounter with God that would be life changing. This message was largely absent in most of the colonies, since for most people in England and America, religion was something inherited from family tradition and was mainly focused on agreeing about certain intellectually agreed upon church doctrines. Whitefield's method was to publicize his coming to towns in the colonies ahead of time and to preach theologically accurate and very passionate sermons in his own style, which was riveting and dynamic. Generally he preached outdoors, so he was not directly connected to specific churches. For him, the only genuine Christianity was regenerate Christianity.

People flocked to hear Whitefield, and thousands, from all denominational backgrounds, experienced the new birth, something most of them knew nothing about until the evangelist came preaching it. Older European (and English) social divisions were based on blood and soil, but these colonials experiencing the new birth together developed a sense of solidarity with one another based on their common experience of salvation. This solidarity crossed denominational lines, since people from different kinds of churches gathered to hear Mr. Whitefield. This new religious identity paved the way for the national revolution that came thirty years later. The revival, known as the Great Awakening, constituted the beginning of America's identity as a nation. As historian Paul Johnson has noted, "The Revolution could not have taken place without this religious background." No Whitefield, no revolution.

Of course, there was a revolution. And that revolution was, in the words of historian Nathan Hatch, "the single most important event in American history." That revolution was necessary, as the British Crown had become increasingly confiscatory of the goods produced by the American colonies. The French and Indian War (or Seven Years' War, 1756–63) was, in effect, the first World War since it was fought on several continents between the British and the French. It left England with a massive war debt, and England then resorted to high taxation on the colonies in attempt to recoup its losses. Many in Parliament agreed with the sentiments of MP Charles Townsend, that the Americans were "Children planted by our Care, nourished up by our Indulgence until they are grown to a Degree of Strength and Opulence, and protected by our arms" (quoted by Thomas Kidd), but who were unwilling to contribute to their own support.

This, of course, was ridiculous! Pampered English lords, waited on by servants, sitting in Parliament wearing powdered wigs had no idea of the travail of Americans on the frontier, carving out a living with their bare hands, bearing their children as they went. The Sugar Act, the Stamp Act, the renewed enforcement of the Navigation Laws, the Townsend Duties, and the Quebec Act all coalesced into one grand attempt at wringing from the colonials every penny possible. And all of this was in violation of English law, which stated clearly that taxes could not be extracted from a people who had no representation in the English Parliament, which the colonies did not have. When American citizens were fired upon by the British in 1775, war for independence became the only option.

Was the Revolutionary War the right thing for the Americans to do? Some critics of the war, both then and now, have argued that the war was unjustifiable. It was just a rebellion based on taxation, and the bloodshed that ensued stands in judgment over the heads of colonials such as Sam Adams, Patrick Henry, George Washington, and others. Some even advanced theological arguments that the war was wrong. John Calvin had contended that revolution was not justifiable, did he not? He did, sort of. John Witherspoon, though, recently arrived in America from Scotland in 1764, reminded people that Calvin had given one exception—if magistrates banding together came to the conclusion that a ruler was acting tyrannically, they could and *should* supplant him, and form a new government. Witherspoon argued that this was exactly what the Continental Congress, which pushed for revolution, was doing. But surely negotiations could have worked out the differences? This is almost certainly not the case. George III was an implacable ruler whose mind was set. Many did seek to move him off his course, but they were unsuccessful. The Revolutionary War for independence had come to a point of inevitability, and what would emerge from that war would be the first modern nation that would stand for "liberty for all." In chapter 6, we will return to that theme.

Conclusion

In this chapter we have surveyed the ideas that several Christian thinkers and churches have held with regard to government along with some key related biblical texts. *Limited* government in this world is the biblical ideal, but that when governments grow too large and begin a heavy-handed practice of extraction of wealth from their people, they inevitably go awry. The Scripture teaches that God is the One to whom we owe ultimate allegiance, but that selfsame God has also instituted governments to keep order in the world. All of those governments are fallen, since we live in a fallen world, and those states might well stand for injustice rather than justice. At times we have to choose whether to obey the state or God, and if we choose God, we may have to pay consequences to the state. Likewise, Augustine articulated that Christians are members of the City of God, but they still dwell in this world. Thomas Aquinas argued in his political theology that there could be a Christian state led by a king, while Calvin contended that a Christian state needed to be headed up by a democratically elected group of men who were wise enough to lead and godly enough to lead for the right reasons. The Puritans brought Calvin's theology to America, but Roger Williams and others (especially the later Baptists), borrowing from Menno Simons and Conrad Grebel and arguing for a free church in a free state, especially contended that government had no right to tell churches how they ought to function or what they ought to believe. Finally, under the preaching of Whitefield, thousands of Americans came to an experience of the new birth together across denominational lines, an experience that made them "Americans," only several decades before they would find themselves testing that new identity in the course of a Revolutionary War with their mother country, England.

Study Questions

1. Which of the biblical texts we have discussed in this chapter call for a limited government?

2. How do Augustine's and Calvin's understanding of government reflect Jesus' statement, "Render to Caesar the things that are Caesar's; and to God the things that are God's"?

3. In what ways can the City of Man incorporate elements of the City of God? In what ways would it be inappropriate for the City of Man to try to be the City of God?

4. Considering some of the texts that we discussed about submission to government, is it ever right for people in a country to foment a revolution? Were Americans in the 1770s justified in revolting against England?

5. Can you think of some contemporary areas where allegiance to the state and allegiance to God might come into conflict?

For Further Reading

Augustine. *The City of God against the Pagans.* Edited and translated by R. W. Dyson. Cambridge: Cambridge University Press, 1998.

Bender, Harold S. *Conrad Grebel, c. 1498–1526: The Founder of the Swiss Brethren Sometimes Called Anabaptists.* Goshen, IN: Mennonite Historical Society, 1950. Reprint, Eugene, OR: Wipf and Stock, 1998.

Foster, Herbert D. "International Calvinism through Locke and the Revolution of 1688." In *The American Historical Review* 32, no. 3 (April 1927): 480–97.

Harrison, Everett F., and Donald A. Hagner. *Romans.* Rev. ed. In Expositor's Bible Commentary 11. Edited by Tremper Longman III and David E. Garland. Grand Rapids: Zondervan, 2007.

Hatch, Nathan O. *The Sacred Cause of Liberty: Republican Thought and the Millennium in Revolutionary New England*. New Haven: Yale University Press, 1977.

Johnson, Paul. *A History of the American People*. New York: HarperCollins, 1997.

Käsemann, Ernst. *New Testament Questions of Today*. Translated by W. J. Montague. London: SCM, 1974. Study edition reprint, 2012.

Kidd, Thomas. *God of Liberty: A Religious History of the American Revolution*. New York: Basic Books, 2010.

Lilla, Mark. *The Stillborn God: Religion, Politics, and the Modern West*. New York: Vintage Books, 2007.

Payton, James R., Jr. *Getting the Reformation Wrong: Correcting Some Misunderstandings*. Downers Grove, IL: InterVarsity, 2010.

Other People's Money | 5

All through history, yet more so in recent centuries, there has been a conversation about the unevenness of wealth and income in the world. As long as there has been civilization, there have been some people (a smaller representation of the population) who have been rich, or at least richer, and then there has been another group (larger, often much larger) who have been, by comparison, poor. In many ancient cultures, the distinction was between a very small group of the superrich, and a very large group of the incredibly poor (at least cash poor), but not much of anybody in between, in what we have come to call the "middle class." This was also true in more recent days, in Europe of the Middle Ages, for instance, when there was a small group of ruling elites who possessed the lion's share of wealth, and then the peasant class (or "serfs") who worked the land and performed other necessary but menial tasks such as blacksmithing, leather-making, and so on.

Today, there is a great deal of discussion about "fairness" in income distribution. President Obama, along with politicians from both sides of the aisle, have made speeches about the "rich" doing their "fair share," by which they mean that federal tax rates ought to be raised another 5 percent or more. These people already pay a much higher tax rate than others, due to our "progressive" tax system that causes the rate of taxation to increase the higher one moves in income. That may be justifiable at some level of argumentation, but most of us would agree that even there a significant disparity ought to be avoided, especially when you consider that the actual amount that "rich" people pay in taxes is significantly higher since they have a higher income. In America today, according to economist Walter Williams, the top 10 percent of earners pay 71 percent of all federal income taxes in this country. Even if you factor in the Social Security and Medicare payroll taxes, the top 10 percent pay 67 percent of all federal taxes on income and payroll!

We will discuss the current situation more later on in this chapter. We have already seen in chapter 4 on government that increasing taxation in the biblical account of Solomon and Rehoboam was done largely for the purpose of expanding the administrative state in Israel and resulted in a bloated government that was unsustainable. As the state extracted more and more from the people, their own wealth plummeted, causing unrest, and eventually, civil war. In this chapter, we will look at the whole issue of income inequality. We will briefly look at some biblical texts that deal with this matter, and we will also examine the question of when and under what circumstances it might be right for government to redistribute wealth from one sector of the economy to another. A few years ago actor Danny DeVito starred as Larry the Liquidator, a corporate raider trying to take over a mom-and-pop company. The title of the film was *Other People's Money*, a title which reminds us that when governments redistribute wealth, for whatever reason, that they are essentially doing it with just that— other people's money.

The Inequality of Wealth

People are entitled to what they have earned. We have already discussed this at some level in chapter 2 as it relates to a theology of work, but there are a few relevant biblical texts that we have not discussed. In the Decalogue, God gave Moses two words that relate to possessions. The eighth commandment is, simply, "You shall not steal." The tenth deals with covetousness: "You shall not covet your neighbor's house; you shall not covet your neighbor's wife or his male servant or his female servant or his ox or his donkey or anything that belongs to your neighbor" (Exod. 20:15, 17 NASB). Both of these commandments are clear and unambiguous. Do not take that which belongs to someone else, and, furthermore, don't even *long* to have that which belongs to others.

There are underlying premises or implications to these commandments. First, having wealth—material things—is not a sin. We have made that point in an earlier chapter, but it bears repeating here. There is nothing intrinsically wrong with people having possessions.

Second, one must not take what belongs to another in order to make it our own. Confiscation of the property of others is a sin. Confiscation, as John Calvin argued, can take several forms (see David W. Hall and Matthew D. Burton, *Calvin and Commerce*). Individual theft is certainly a sin, but Calvin also argued that forced redistribution of wealth by the state was nothing short of *legalized theft*. Calvin recognized that any society would contain people who were poor, or even very poor, and that such people would need help. This was certainly true of the refugee-saturated Geneva. The Reformer organized what he called the *Bourse Française*, a body of deacons, who bore the responsibility of assisting those in distress (see Bruce Gordon, *Calvin*). Their strategy was multi-layered. They offered job training for those who did not possess skills to work in city employment. They examined cases of those who were requesting financial assistance, and they found ways to provide that assistance when the need was genuine. This assistance did not come from city taxation, but from church offerings given for that very purpose, and from individual philanthropy. The churches and individuals of Geneva were able to handle many thousands of needs by a network of services, but there was no *coerced* confiscation.

A third implication of the two commandments cited above is that not only must we not take from others forcefully, but we must also avoid the temptation of *wishing* we might have what they own. Efforts at enforced redistribution, whether by personal or legalized theft, often arise from either the desire of one group to have more, or from the desire of another group to see to it that the *poor* have more. This latter approach has become quite common in modern times, as Socialists and Social Democrats have lobbied for more and more legislation to take higher tax revenues from the wealthier persons in society and to redistribute that wealth to the "less fortunate."

Franklin Delano Roosevelt constitutes a classic example of this redistributive philosophy. Campaigning for president in 1932, he gave a speech on "The Forgotten Man," a phrase that owed its origin to William Graham Sumner of Yale, who had asserted that in politics and taxation where redistribution of wealth was part of the goal, the "forgotten man" was the taxpayer whose income is taken and then given to others who are in some need. FDR, however, inverted the original story, as Amity Shlaes documents in her helpful book, claiming that the "forgotten man" was the man in the soup line in the Great Depression, which was raging then at the time of the presidential campaign. The phrase "grew legs," as they say, and the "forgotten man" of FDR's speech became a campaign slogan that helped him defeat Herbert Hoover in the election. Sumner, we are convinced, had it right and FDR got it wrong. The real forgotten man is the man who has to foot the bill when some person or group of persons, A, sees another person or group, B, in need and calls for redistribution of wealth. It is actually then another person, C, whose income is *redistributed* to make that happen. We can covet others' goods for our own gain, or we can covet to have a sense of satisfaction that someone else is getting "justice" by giving what he has to others, but it is *coveting* nonetheless.

Further, it needs to be noted that in politics, this "coveting on behalf of someone else" is rarely done on humanitarian grounds. There are of course philanthropic agencies that do have a passion to help the poor, but by the time it gets to the political realm, even though it is presented in humanitarian terms, it is often (usually) a vehicle for one group to exercise political power. We will illustrate this tendency later in this chapter.

The Justice of Redistribution

Let us look at redistribution of wealth by examining a few historical examples. People living in the city of Rome often did little work at all (except of course the slaves), but the patrician class of Roman citizens was generally quite wealthy by the standards of the time. The Roman emperors wanted Rome to be a large city, for purposes of prestige and grandiose display of their own greatness, so they extended offers to wealthy persons to move to Rome. They "sweetened the pot" by providing large amounts of free food to the citizens of Rome. Grain was imported from conquered Africa, while wine and oil were brought from conquered Spain and Gaul. Between two hundred and four hundred tons of grain were shipped to Rome every year, grain taken by Roman tax collectors (called in the New Testament, "publicans") from farmers as their "contribution" to the empire that had conquered them. The oil and wine shipments to the city amounted to about 750 shiploads per year. In the third century, pork was added to the "entitlement," and thus the citizens of Rome were parodied with names such as "Piglet" and "Sausage" by those living in the provinces. Historian Raymond Van Dam comments that "the food supply of Rome had become, literally, pork barrel politics."

The benefits were not limited to food. Games were also a part of the prerequisites for living in the city. Emperor Trajan staged massive gladiatorial spectacles at what was called "Circus Maximus." After his army defeated the Dacians, the emperor presented games at Rome that lasted 123 consecutive days, featuring combats between ten thousand gladiators, and that saw the slaughter of about eleven thousand animals. Bread and circus! All of this was virtually free of charge to the people whose homes lay inside the walls of the city of Rome. The purpose, as we have already indicated, was to present to the world the greatness that was Rome, both to awe them into submission and to hint to them that one day, if they played their cards right, they might share in something of this glory. But they never would. For one thing, this glory was completely focused on the city and on the emperors themselves, and for another thing, by the third century AD the economic foundations of the great city began to crumble under the load of trying to administer this unwieldy administrative state.

It is impossible to justify such grandiose redistribution of wealth from the provinces to the capital simply for the purpose of glorifying an empire. But one might make a case for forced redistribution of wealth for humanitarian purposes. Keep in mind that we are talking about *forced* redistribution; this is not a matter of passing a hat around and asking people for contributions. With Rome the tax collectors took one-third of what people grew on their farms. The military and police power of the state was at their service if farmers resisted or tried to cheat. You don't cheat Rome! In the modern situation the federal and state governments deduct money from most people's paychecks in the form of income tax, and then redistribute a certain amount of that money to lower-income people, to "qualified" people who have no other access to health care insurance, to the unemployed, to people who qualify for certain programs, and to some families that qualify for an extra cash payment from the government even if they themselves paid no federal income taxes (something oddly called, "Earned Income Credit").

Is such redistribution justifiable? Money forcibly taken from some people and given to others? I think at *some level* it is. We live in a large country with a complicated network of federal, state, county, and municipal governments, with some of those more local governments very strapped for resources. There ought to be some level of welfare available to the extremely needy. Earlier in American (and world) history those things were taken care of by family, church, and civic philanthropic organizations, as Marvin Olasky has demonstrated in his very helpful book, *The Tragedy of American Compassion*. Before about 1820 in America help for the needy was pretty much all taken care of by family and church. Cotton Mather in Massachusetts had once argued for governmental help for the poor, but of course for Mather government and church were closely linked together, something that began to unwind with the affirmation of the Bill of Rights and the Constitution. (Massachusetts maintained a state-church system until 1831.) From about 1820 until about 1890 philanthropy was carried out by family, church, and civic organizations in many major cities. After about 1890 the federal government slowly took on more and more of the welfare responsibility.

There needs to be a safety net for the truly needy. But over the years that safety net has been used for an increasingly *larger* segment of society. A new report has just come out of the federal government that now 35 percent of Americans are recipients of welfare. Fifty years ago that number stood at 6 percent. Approximately 100 million Americans now receive aid from the federal government, according to Robert Rector of the Heritage

Foundation. There are eighty different federal programs for administering this aid, and in the last fiscal year they gave away a total of $927 billion. As of July 2012, over 22 million American households were on Food Stamps (SNAP), an all-time high, a number that translates to almost 60 million Americans, or slightly less than one in five.

In 1996 then sitting president Bill Clinton worked with Republicans in Congress to reform our nation's costly welfare system, enacting a bill that in Clinton's words would restore "America's basic bargain of providing opportunity and demanding in return, responsibility." The new law simply required that anyone receiving welfare assistance in only *three* of the eighty programs (mentioned above) must also look for and find work. Our nation was established on the idea that people would work hard and enjoy the fruits of their labors. After the passage of that bill in 1996, the percentage of single mothers with a job grew from 58 to 75 percent in less than a decade. It was hugely successful! Yet now the current Department of Health and Human Services has negated this hugely successful initiative, turning the clock back on years of successful bipartisan efforts. Federal assistance has mushroomed from being nearly nonexistent in the late 1800s to being a major part of the government's budget in 2012.

How many of those receiving this assistance are actually the very poor? In 2011 the Census Bureau reported that 46 million Americans were poor. But the same Census Bureau also reported that 80 percent of these poor households have air conditioning, nearly three-fourths have a car or truck and 31 percent have two vehicles, and nearly two-thirds have cable or satellite television. In addition, half have a personal computer and one in seven have more than one computer, with nearly half of them going online. One-third have a large screen plasma or LCD television. One-fourth have a digital recording system, such as a TiVo, and more than half have video game systems. Less than 10 percent of the poor live in mobile homes or trailers. When Lyndon Johnson pushed through the "Great Society" legislation in the 1960s, his goal was to make poverty a thing of the past. Judged by that goal, the Great Society was a Gigantic Failure!

It seems clear that the approach taken by many in Washington is the polar opposite of the position taken by historic Americans. Americans in the past crossed rugged mountain ranges, barged down the Ohio, crossed the seemingly interminable western plains, and eked out a living in hard and intractable lands. People sailed the tumultuous Atlantic and launched an "Errand in the Wilderness" to have something of their own. These people did not want to depend on government. When the Rockefellers and the Carnegies built their companies, they asked for no help from government, in part because they knew that government is easily corruptible, and they wanted no part of what we will discuss a bit later as "crony capitalism."

Remember, when the government spends money, that financial assistance has to come from somewhere. We talked in chapter 4 about how when the Queen of Sheba gave Solomon all of that gold, it came from somewhere. It came from *someone(s)*. There is a clear link between Solomon's extraction of wealth from fruitful people to use in building his empire and the moral weakness, decay, and corruption that resulted in his life and the life of his sons. I recently pastored a church in eastern Kentucky where the coal industry has been virtually shut down by government regulators, in a county where now 20 percent of the people are unemployed and are on the government dole. The deleterious effects on morale, on parenting, on sexual morals, on drug trafficking, on alcoholism, and a hundred other maladies are the worst I have seen in all my years of ministry. Here are people, living on other people's money, and all it does is drive them into moral decay.

The government tries to portray itself as the savior of such people. While it can and should help *some* very poor for a temporary period, with the goal of helping them once again to become fruitful, the fact is that this is not the way welfare has played out in America. The government produces nothing, so it has to get the money from somewhere, or from someone. That "someone" is productive Americans (and their businesses), the "forgotten man" who will have to be taxed at ever-higher rates in order to provide this "safety net" on which people are becoming more and more dependent.

But other people's money is not taken just to provide welfare for the poor.

Engineering a New Society

Twelve years ago the federal government's budget was a little below 20 percent of the nation's overall Gross Domestic Product (the entire amount that our nation produces, measured in dollars in a single year), a number that is still remarkably high. (In 1910 the federal budget was about 2 percent of the GDP.) In 2012 the federal budget is 25 percent of GDP. That is not all due to welfare spending; in fact, much of it is simply due to the expansion of the size of the federal bureaucracy under President Barack Obama, whose administration has created over 220,000 new federal jobs, tens of thousands of them in the six-figure income range. It also expanded greatly under President George W. Bush, who created a whole new bureaucracy, the Department of Homeland Security, after the 9/11 plane attacks in 2001.

Perhaps we need a Department of Homeland Security. That is certainly a debatable issue. But increasingly government spending is going to other causes. The Environmental Protection Agency (EPA) has raised the cost for coal extraction by imposing fees and newer regulations that make it difficult for the coal industry to be profitable, even though coal-generated energy is as safe and as environmentally friendly as any other source. There are projections that as many as 175 coal-fired energy plants will go offline in 2013. This has resulted in a sharp rise in the cost of electricity, passed on to the consumer, and has contributed to unemployment as many coal workers have been laid off. Higher fees and costlier regulations have also been imposed on the oil industry as well as a ban for a period of time on offshore drilling in the Gulf of Mexico. When the EPA issues a new regulation that contaminants in some form of air or water technology need to be reduced from twelve parts per billion to one part per billion (and that is happening right now), and the new machine to make that happen will cost hundreds of thousands of dollars, what sense does that make? When conservatives respond that this is simply not cost-effective, they are told that they all want "dirtier water and dirtier air."

President Obama has said as much as this, when as Campaigner Obama in 2008 he made speeches stating that the cost of energy would have to rise in order to make way for "renewable" sources of energy, such as solar, wind, and others. Why? Solar energy has been around for decades, but it has not developed the capability to provide the amount of energy needed to meet our nation's vast energy needs. So what is the solution? The Obama administration has worked to guarantee loans to companies that are trying to find more productive ways to utilize renewable energy. One of those was the solar power company Solyndra, which received over $500 million in federally backed loans. That company went out of business in 2011, and corporate records show that even at the time that the federally guaranteed loans were negotiated, the company was in dire financial shape. It was later also disclosed that the company and its executives had given generously to Obama's 2008 campaign for the presidency. One cannot help but see this as the very kind of crony capitalism that Rockefeller, Carnegie, and others saw as the key to the demise of American entrepreneurship. Republican and Democratic administrations both succumb to the temptations of crony capitalism. A commitment to supporting business is not the same as a commitment to reinvigorating American entrepreneurship.

Why make this point? Because, as in welfare expansion, this kind of crony capitalism is being financed with other people's money—your money and mine! At a time when unemployment in our nation is over 8 percent, when small companies are going out of business at record rates, should the federal government be *artificially* causing the price of energy to skyrocket? Should the federal government be choosing winners and losers in the economic system because of its own philosophy about what constitutes good sources of energy and bad? If a new technology really is a good technology and if it has merit as providing the kind of energy our nation really needs, won't it prove its worth on its own merit? When John Rockefeller and others discovered oil fields in Pennsylvania and Ohio in the 1850s and discovered that they could distill a substance called kerosene out of the crude oil, then found a way to manufacture, market, and distribute that kerosene, they provided Americans with something they desperately needed and did it at a price that everyone could afford. They did it all *without* government help or the need to get the government to tax other people so they could develop a product that would make them wealthy.

Much has been made of how people can't really be successful without government help. And it is true, that for the *most part* the government has built roads, bridges, canals, and even railroads to facilitate commerce. That decision was made in the 1820s, urged on by Kentucky congressman and senator Henry Clay. The Congress decided that these were the contributions that government could make, thus facilitating everyone's possibility for "the pursuit of happiness" in this country. But that is a far cry from federally guaranteed loans to a company that was far, far from being able to produce a resource that would make a difference in the lives of Americans in the near future.

Or take another issue, one that is related to energy but that takes on its own level of importance: global warming, or what is now being called "climate change." According to the legislative director of environmental activist group Greenpeace, "We are running out of sky, not oil." Thirty years ago scientists were talking about "global cooling" and the coming new ice age. Then it turns out they were wrong and we are all going to slowly roast to death. In 2010 emails were released that showed that scientists at some institutions knew that they were hyping what was really going on and not telling the truth about their research. They knew that man-made global warming was largely a hoax.

What thousands of recent scientists who have no "dog in the hunt" have concluded is that there is no way that human activity can affect the climate in any significant manner. (Meteorologists are the one group most opposed to the current claims about global warming, which is significant to say the least.) Other factors contribute 98 percent of the various influences that lead to climate change, leaving 2 percent (actually less than 2 percent) to human activities. Devoting the kind of technological and financial resources in the way that people like Al Gore have called for would bankrupt the economies of the world and plunge the planet into a financial depression unlike anything it has ever seen before. Unfortunately, many people, including many Christians, have been lured to buy into the notion that stewardship of the planet means that we have to support the call by "experts" and by the federal government to support the kind of coercive (both financially and in terms of our freedoms) programs and policies being called for. In a forthcoming work *Seeking the City*, my coauthor, Tom Pratt, and I have this to say about such coercion: "No more destructive program has been conceived by world politicians since the *takeover of the Soviet Union* in 1917. It is this realization that has caused some pundits to label the advocates of this so-called 'green revolution,' 'watermelons'—meaning they are green on the outside and red on the inside." The heat of the debate comes from the panicky slogans offered by climate change advocates that simply invite rhetorical response.

Lurking behind all of this is the very real fact that huge amounts of money are tied into the "science" of climate change. This money is in the form of research grants for universities that do the kind of studies that supposedly substantiate the claims of climate change science. The "Climategate" emails mentioned earlier are probably only the tip of the iceberg of experts hiding the real truths about the matter. Contracts for wind power turbines, federally backed loans for green energy research and production, tax credits for people who buy electric automobiles or solar panels for their homes—all of this is paid for with *other people's money*! Yours and mine! Corporations seek governmental favor ("rents") to stifle competition and thus create for themselves monopolies in a variety of different industries. This is really nothing other than "corporate welfare." For Christians, Jesus' various parables, as well as the Old Testament prophets' withering blasts against wealthy people colluding together to prevent justice from being done to the rest of society, ought to ring in our ears when we read about companies currying special favors from the government.

But even more problematic than the grab for money on the part of people who are attempting to get rich by sidling up to the government is the fact that all of this, at its heart, is a grab for *power* on the part of politicians. The attempt to get more people hooked on welfare (more votes?), the effort to control the energy portion of the American economy, and all the rest is a play for power in politics. Certainly this can be a problem on both sides of the political aisle, and I have about as many criticisms of Republican presidents and politicians over the last fifty years as I do of their Democratic counterparts. But the real problem is that politicians are in a mad dash for political power, and they can only be reined in by the people by throwing them out of office when they grab for too much. This power is nowhere more obvious and evident than in the power of the government to tax at will. You can say what you will about Rockefeller, Carnegie, and the other so-called robber barons; I would rather be at their mercy than at the mercy of an all-powerful administrative state!

Conclusion

In this chapter we have attempted to detail through history the approach of governments to appropriate the money of the wealthy class and to use it for their own purposes. Some welfare is necessary in a large and populated nation, but despite the fact that we are not in an "extreme" situation (for instance, a humanitarian crisis or devastation), we are nonetheless being exploited by the federal government. Government often levies heavy taxes in order to extend its power. Rome was fascist in this respect as was seventeenth-century France (as we will see in the next chapter), and it is becoming hard not to see that America may be going the same way, that is, unless we have some kind of deep and abiding change at the top. Take a lesson from the stories of Ahab, Solomon, and Rehoboam of the Old Testament. Governments that confiscate from one class of society for their own purposes only create moral and fiscal problems—they solve nothing.

Study Questions

1. What two of the Ten Commandments ought to make us stop and reconsider redistribution of wealth? How should those commands make Christians think about the American welfare system?

2. John Rockefeller and Andrew Carnegie built massive companies and financial empires, and they did it without government help. Do you think they should have worked closer with the government?

3. Should the federal government offer loan guarantees to companies that may be working to create forms of renewable energy, or should it leave that up to investors?

4. We talked about the "forgotten man" in this chapter. Who is the "forgotten man" in our nation today?

5. To what degree should American people today be dependent on the federal government? What about these issues: income, health care, childcare, education, old-age care?

For Further Reading

DiLorenzo, Thomas J. *How Capitalism Saved America: The Untold History of Our Country, from the Pilgrims to the Present.* New York: Three Rivers, 2005.

Horner, Christopher C. *Red Hot Lies: How Global Warming Alarmists Use Threats, Fraud, and Deception to Keep You Misinformed.* Washington, DC: Regnery, 2008.

Olasky, Marvin. *The Tragedy of American Compassion.* Washington: Regnery Gateway, 1992. Distributed by National Book Network.

Rector, Robert. The Heritage Foundation. http://www.heritage.org/. See publications by the author.

Shlaes, Amity. *The Forgotten Man: A New History of the Great Depression.* New York: HarperCollins, 2007.

Sowell, Thomas. "The Paul Ryan Choice." RealClearPolitics. August 14, 2012. http://www.realclearpolitics.com/articles/2012/08/14/the _paul_ryan_choice_115088.html.

Van Dam, Raymond. *Rome and Constantinople: Rewriting Roman History during Late Antiquity.* Waco, TX: Baylor University Press, 2010.

Political Economy | 6

I n this chapter we will discuss the rise and development of "political economy." That term may be new to you, but it is not that difficult to understand. It is a term that refers to the simple fact that in any given nation or state, governing structures adopt a certain way to relate to the economy. Or they choose none and simply let the economy alone. We have gestured at this several times already in the previous five chapters of our study, but here we will be more specific about the historical development of political economy, its relation to religion and to the state, and we will then ask some pragmatic questions about how we should relate to all of that in our personal and church lives. This chapter is the most philosophical of the preceding five, but we will do our best to keep it understandable.

Keep in mind our previous discussions about theology of work, theology of wealth, and political theology. Much of that will come to a head in this chapter's discussion of political economy.

Political Economy in Developing
Europe: Manorialism

We have already discussed Rome and its relation to its provinces at the level of taxation and power, so we will not need to cover that ground again, except to note a few things. Rome was a *fascist* state that extended a heavy hand of control over the economy of the provinces, it taxed at will, and its only point of weakness, from our standpoint in history, was its unwieldy size and the deplorable state of communications at that time in history. In other words, these facts constituted weaknesses in the Roman state's ability to exercise total control because it could not *get* to everyone and it did not *know* everything that a modern, industrialized, technological government might know about its people.

What do we mean by "fascist"? There is a symbol that many of you have seen. It is a bunch of sticks bundled together with an axe, with cords tying them all in one bundle. This is called the "fasces." The message is that a group of small sticks, representing weaker nations, is bound together with an axe, representing a very powerful nation. As long as the bundle remains intact, nothing happens; all is well. But if the smaller sticks seek to unravel the bundle, the axe will fall. Fascism is, thus, the power of an overweening state exercising its will on weaker states and on the populace to carry out its will, no matter what. At one time, "Fascism" was a neutral term, just representing a form of governmental leadership and direction. Because in the twentieth century the primary Fascist states were Nazi Germany and Mussolini's Italy, the term has taken on a bad connotation. It is still a term applicable, however, to any state (or government) that attempts to exercise its will and to use the power of coercion to ensure that it gets its way. We will examine several examples of Fascism in this chapter.

After Rome "fell," hundreds of petty "kingdoms" dotted the "European" landscape. Led by lords who often were just a step or two above the poor conditions of their subjects, many of them over time developed political economies in which peasants (serfs) had a small plot of land that they were allowed to work and a small collection of livestock for the maintenance of their families, from which they paid to the lord "rents in kind." They also were obligated to work the lord's land, and over time this led to the increasing wealth of the local lords. The lord ruled from his "manor," thus giving to this economic system the name "manorial," though it is sometimes mistakenly called "feudal." The term *feudal* actually referred to the military relationship that barons, knights, and others had to their liege, usually a king or a prince, one or two more steps up the social ladder. They usually were bound to give him thirty or forty days a year of their lives if they were needed in war.

The average European (or Englishman) during this time in history lived lives so utterly filled with drudgery and monotony that it is beyond our ability even to grasp. Every day was pretty much a copy of the day before. Only the change of the seasons brought any alterations, and those were minor. Children of today who complain about being bored need to spend a day in the life of a peasant boy or girl from the year AD 900 or so. This manorial economic system with its repetitive and monotonous tasks prevailed in much of Western Europe and England until well into the sixteenth century, and still remained in some places long after that. We sometimes think that economic, political, and historical realities (and religious ones) suddenly go through a transformation and big changes happen overnight. This is seldom true, and century transitions usually mean nothing. The life of most people in Europe changed little if at all for the thousand years from AD 500 to AD 1500. The lord governed his people, made decisions (along with bishops) to adjudicate disputes, demanded work from his serfs, went off to war with some regularity (usually in the spring), and life went drearily on.

A sign of some change came with the Crusades. Europeans went to *Outremer* (French for "over the sea," their name for the

Middle East) to rescue their Christian brothers from being slaughtered by the new Islamic force known as the Seljuk Turks first in AD 1096 (see Rodney Stark, *God's Battalions*). Islam had been around since the early seventh century, and by the early eighth century had conquered most of the Middle East, North Africa, most of Spain, and held toeholds in coastal areas of Italy and France, and some of the islands in the Mediterranean. There had been some amount of peace between the Muslims and the Christians, especially after the Battle of Tours, which was discussed in chapter 2. The Crusades brought thousands of European soldiers (and others) into *Outremer*, and that would change everything. Once they were there, soldiers quickly acquired a taste for coffee, tobacco, pepper, silk, spices, and many other commodities previously unknown to them. Although the Western Kingdom of Jerusalem would last less than a century (from 1099–1185, when Saladin defeated the Christian forces), trade opened up between East and West that would eventually make first the Italian city-states wealthy and, over time, more and more of Europe. This wealth, along with the increasing depletion of the noble class through war in the various Crusades (eight in all), resulted in the rise of something that looked kind of like the modern European nations. (Much of this is told in Peter Heather, *Empires and Barbarians*.)

Still, things changed little. There was a king in France in, say, AD 1200, but he probably knew little of his own country. After 1066 and the Battle of Hastings, the English were ruled by the Normans, descendants of Vikings who had relocated to Western France a century before. Yet William the Conqueror did not even live in the country he now ruled but returned to Normandy. Local rule by barons, dukes, and various lords was still the real reality in people's lives. Manorialism with its drudgery was still the prevailing system under which most people lived their daily lives. Of course, if you have never known anything else, perhaps you might not complain too much.

Mercantilist Economics:
Who's Got the Most Gold?

The discovery of the New World brought more rapid changes. Portuguese and Spanish discoveries of gold and silver in Central and South America created a passion for the precious metals that set off war and piracy and a rush on the part of the lagging French, Dutch, and English to get in on the new wealth. The new wealth brought about the first real shift in political economy in a thousand years, as the increasingly wealthy nations of Europe witnessed the rise of a merchant class in places outside Italy, connected to the new wealth. Kings had war chests, literally, that were filled with gold and silver bullion. These war chests enabled them to purchase cannons (a relatively new technology) and muskets, to hire large armies (with the feudal system of liege and vassal now fading into the past), and to purchase luxury items from abroad. Our image of the warring European nations from books by people like Sir Walter Scott (*Ivanhoe*, *The Talisman*, and so on) was finally coming into focus. This new form of political economy, mercantilism, was based on the view that the nation with the most gold is the wealthiest nation. (For documentation on this section, see books such as Stephen R. Brown, *Merchant Kings*.)

But the rapid accumulation of precious metals had an unintended side effect. Since there was so much gold in the market, the price of goods began to skyrocket in Spain and Portugal. I mean, if the money is there, why not charge more? And merchants did just that. Price inflation essentially wiped out much of the benefit that the government had accrued from the accumulation of the new specie (gold and silver). Still, the newly expanding merchant class did bring about a marked *change* in the economic system of Europe.

What about the other nations, specifically Holland and England? They were unable to match Spain's exploitation of the South American gold fields, since their holdings in North America and the Caribbean were not rich in those minerals, at least not until gold in California and Alaska was discovered much later. But they matched the transition to merchant economies by different routes. The Dutch seized control of the spice trade from the Portuguese. Portugal had earlier developed navigation technologies that enabled them to sail their ships beyond the sight of land and so had lunged ahead of the other European nations in the all-important trade with other parts of the world. Under Admiral Alfonso de Albuquerque, Portugal early on had taken control of the crucial Spice Islands in Indonesia, five small islands that were, at the time, the only place in the world where nutmeg, mace, and cloves grew. These spices had long been sought by people all over the world, not for the purpose of adding flavor to food and drink, but for their *odorous* qualities in a day when bathing was rare and deodorants were unavailable. Placing cloves or nutmeg in little bags and attaching them to clothing made riding a long distance in a warm carriage a much more *pleasant* activity! The Portuguese, for the first time in hundreds of years of searching, had finally located the Spice Islands, and had wrested control of them away from native Indonesians for financial profit, since the trade was *very* lucrative.

Portugal's tiny population, however, had made it difficult to maintain its edge, and in the late 1500s the Dutch had taken over the spice trade. Who needs to control the gold mines of Peru when you have control of a market that would enable you to get the gold by another means? The Dutch also moved into North America (New Holland) and began a vigorous trade venture with Native Americans around the Great Lakes for furs. Europe had long depleted its fur trade, but increasingly wealthy Europeans had a lust for coats, hats, and other garments made from the pelts of animals. In the early seventeenth century the Dutch virtually cornered the market, but by the latter third of that century they would lose their North American holdings to the English king, Charles II. In the 1660s Charles routed the Dutch out of New

Holland and then placed the new land under the direction of his brother, James, Duke of York, who promptly named the new colony after himself! In the seventeenth century the English further developed the North American colonies in producing tobacco, timber (much needed in Europe), cod fishing (in New England), furs, and in other ways. This enabled them to trade with the Spanish and other gold-procuring nations. All of this, along with a remarkable rise in sheep raising in England, resulted in that nation becoming the world economic leader by the eighteenth century. That in turn led to further British colonialism and a slogan: "The sun never sets on the British Empire."

What should be obvious from this brief survey is that the rise of economic fortune for the Europeans was the increase in *trade*. Trade, throughout history, has been the key to economic development. The Romans knew this, and they sought to control every aspect of trade. The Italian city-states came to understand this during and after the Crusades, and their significant control of much of the Mediterranean trade resulted in such things as the Italian Renaissance, since the rise of a literate and cultured society is dependent on the ability of a significant class of people to have leisure time, and that only happens when people do not have to spend every waking hour eking out a living. The European states of the sixteenth and seventeenth centuries also understood this, and sought in various ways to control trade, from cornering markets, piracy, burning one another's ships while in harbor, enacting heavy tariffs on imports, and a thousand other avenues. Since, in the mercantilist understanding of economics, whoever has the most gold and silver is the wealthiest (in a sense), trade *is* war! If you are Spain, you want to export but not import, since imports require the relinquishing of gold in order to pay for those products. So trade has to be heavily controlled from the top down.

The most extreme example of controlling trade from the top down can be seen in France under King Louis XIV. When he came to the throne he inherited a finance minister from the man who had been his regent, Cardinal Mazarin, a genius of a man named Jean-Baptiste Colbert. Colbert's aim was to make France the *greatest nation* in the world and to do so by meticulous management of *every* aspect of the French economy. The first step in launching such a venture was to control *information*. Max Weber has noted that state paperwork engendered the need for bureaucracy, which can be defined as "the exercise of control on the basis of knowledge." To centralize a government one first had to identify its archives and to centralize them. A person in a sufficient position of authority might then control the flow of information—all information, potentially—and thereby control the entire economy. This was Colbert's aim, and he established a strategy for doing this at every possible level. (Much of this material is taken from Jacob Soll, *The Information Master*.)

Colbert employed the assistance of intellectuals, merchants, military men, and a host of others in his scheme to have the Crown dominate *every* area of French cultural and political life. He used intellectuals to develop an intricate system of espionage that enabled him to follow the movements and machinations of nobles, of foreign sailing vessels, of merchants in the colonies, and of church officials, in essence forming "a centralized, internal corps of professional state observers whose writings would have concrete results." Only the *Jesuits* had ever worked harder to formulate a system of espionage like that developed by Colbert. Indeed, Colbert himself had trained early on to be a Jesuit priest.

But there were other issues for Colbert. In mercantilist economics it is expedient for the government to be in control of the economy of the *nation* as well, to the degree that it could. Colbert built France into the one nation of its time that was actually capable of doing so, far more than England, Holland, or the previously strong but now much weakened Spain. Much of this had to do with the previously noted absolutism that underlay Louis's policies. France had nothing similar to the English *Magna Carta*, a regulative device that limited the authority of the monarch in that country. The French *Parlement* held much less authority than its English counterpart, due both to the constitutions of France and to recent history. All of this allowed Colbert to run roughshod, with virtually no restraint.

Colbert's accumulation and control of data was enormous. He kept elaborate "inventories, scrapbooks, journals, and ledgers for each tax farmer, region, different tax and different royal expenditure." He required his assistants to master double-entry bookkeeping and to manage all national, regional, and district accounting data using that method. He built his own library to be second in size only to the Royal Library, and there, along with an extensive book collection, he kept all his notebooks, journals, and folders containing the data his agents had amassed in their efforts to catalogue the economy, the travels of nobles, the state of foreign trade, and information of foreign domestic life—hundreds of thousands of individual documents and collections of material, all of it organized in such a way that he, the Information Master, could put his hands on just the required piece of paper or ledger within moments. The nineteenth-century editor of Colbert's papers offered his opinion that Colbert was truly obsessed with knowing, literally, *everything* that could be known about every nook and cranny of the large and expansive French countryside and city life in the twenty-two years that he served Louis XIV. This is *fascist* government control of a mercantilist economy at its best, or worst! But something new was on the horizon.

It Started with Adam: The Free Market

Isn't it odd that up to this point in history, no philosopher had written about what people do to make a living? In 1776 a moral philosopher in Glasgow, Scotland, published a book that would change the way Europeans and Americans thought about the economy. His name was Adam Smith, and in that year he published a very large book with the title *An Inquiry into the Nature and Causes of the Wealth of Nations*. Economics as a discipline had been around a long time, dating back at least to the Catholic scholastic authors of the thirteenth century, and anticipated even as far back as Plato and Aristotle. But Smith's work came along at a time when the wealth of European nations actually was *growing*, and not just because of increased trade with the East and the discovery of gold in the Western Hemisphere. By the middle of the eighteenth century a revolution in the development of *technology* had begun to transform England. This "revolution" was due mostly to the rise of modern natural science that had begun in earnest a century earlier. People like Francis Bacon, Nicolaus Copernicus, Sir Isaac Newton, Robert Boyle, Galileo Galilei, and a host of others had transformed the way educated people thought about the natural world. By 1750 new looming and spinning machines were capitalizing on the English sheep industry, making English wool by far the cheapest in the world. In the next several decades, steam engines, the cotton gin, and a host of other mechanical inventions would transform manufacturing first in England, then in America, and by the middle of the nineteenth century in many other European nations. Smith's book *coincided* with this transformation. Prior to his book, six thousand years of human history had passed "without a seminal work being published on the subject that dominated every waking hour of practically every human being: making a living" (Mark Skousen, *The Making of Modern Economics*).

Smith's *basic* ideology can be easily summed up, even though his tome was nearly a thousand pages long. He believed in *free trade*, the *division of labor*, and the development of *industrial technology*. Throughout the book Smith advocated the principle of "natural liberty," which meant, for him, that people ought to have the freedom to do what they want with little interference from the state, so long as they are law-abiding citizens. This is especially the case with reference to economic decisions. Smith believed that economic freedom was a basic human *liberty*, a view that he held in common with John Locke, who affirmed that we have inalienable rights to life, liberty, and the pursuit of *property*. In *Wealth of Nations*, Smith argued, "To prohibit a great people . . . from making all that they can of every part of their own produce, or from employing their stock and industry in the way that they judge most advantageous to themselves, is a manifest violation of the most sacred rights of mankind." This Scottish philosopher made it his point to stand up for those rights. This book and the conversation it launched was the most important development in the modern philosophical discussion over free-market economics, or, though the term would not be coined for almost another century after Smith, *capitalism*.

"Natural liberty" then was the key to economic development and the rising wealth of nations. Whereas mercantilists previously believed accumulation of gold was the key to the wealth of nations, Smith said that the key was natural liberty. *Turn people loose* with new technologies and *see what they can do*. This gave to enterprising inventors the sense that they could develop new ways of doing things and not have to *battle* incessantly with the *government* to be able to implement their new ideas. There were, in addition, two other elements that we will discuss briefly. The first issue is *competition*. Smith writes, "Every man, as long as he does not violate the laws of justice, is left perfectly free to pursue his own interest his own way, and to bring both his industry and capital into competition with those of any other man, or order of men." Individuals in Smith's perspective have the right to compete with one another in the production and exchange of goods and services. Competition, in Smith's view, is a sign of a *healthy* economy. There are several *threats* to competition, most of which are represented by the two regular sources of difficulty Smith had already identified:

government and protectionist trade *guilds* or *unions*. The *greatest threat* to fruitfulness comes when the two of these *collude* to stifle competition. When government prefers one company against another or provides trade guilds with excessive protectionism, trade is no longer *free*, and the net effect is that prosperity to some sectors of the economy comes because they obtain governmental favor, for whatever reason. We have previously referred to this as *corporate welfare*, and it had stifled economic growth for centuries before Smith. The government should act as an "invisible hand" that encourages and enables all who wish to be prosperous, but not as a *visible hand* that helps and enables only some. The net effect of that kind of policy is that consumers pay higher prices for goods, unemployment becomes systemic, and the overall economy suffers.

So then, is this all just automatic? If the government allows for a level playing field, will prosperity just happen? This raises the second issue about Smith's approach that must be emphasized. Smith believed that prosperity would only come about if there were a general commitment to *moral business transactions* in society. There needed to be a shared societal ethic that emphasized honesty in advertising, integrity in business, fair treatment of employees, and other kinds of moral standards, standards that reflect the ethical approach to business transactions that we spoke about in our previous discussion regarding money and wealth in the Bible (see chap. 3). Smith did not claim to be articulating a "Christian" view of economics, but his exposition in the *Wealth of Nations* contained many principles that are consistent with biblical morality. This needs to be emphasized because some critics, like Max Weber whom we have mentioned before, have accused the Scottish philosopher of condoning greed, egotism, and Western-style decadence. When Gordon Gekko in the film *Wall Street* says, "Greed, for lack of a better word, is good," some would see in that comment an echo of Adam Smith. Nothing could be further from the truth!

What he, in effect, was saying is consistent with Luther's, Calvin's, and the Puritans' view of vocation. Smith believed in *limited government*, the very thing we have seen is consistent with the Bible and its critique of the Solomonic/Rehoboamistic expanding and extracting style of government that only ends in moral decay and dissolution. By contrast Smith's system assures that both buyer and seller benefit from every *voluntary* transaction; otherwise the transaction would not take place. Transactions in an economic system must be governed by a general systemic commitment to moral values and integrity.

Although it is merely a coincidence of history that Smith's book was published the very year that American leaders signed the Declaration of Independence, that accident was to develop into a curious kind of *synchronicity*. By the time the Revolutionary War was over, the Treaty of Paris had been signed, and the thirteen new states had carried on their brief flirtation with confederacy as a governing model, in 1787 the delegates from each state meeting in Philadelphia signed on to a new kind of federal government. By the time the details had been spelled out, the United States of America became the first nation in the world founded on four foundational principles of freedom: freedom of *speech* (and press), freedom of *markets*, *free elections* (for those with the franchise, which was limited at first), and completely free exercise of *religion*. In a real sense Adam Smith's philosophy had found a more congenial home in America than even in his own Britain. But over the coming decades not everyone would be happy with this new economic philosophy.

Heretics and Wafflers: Marx and Keynes

Karl Marx was born to a Jewish family in Prussia in 1818, a family that had converted to Lutheranism in part to advance his father's career as a lawyer. He studied philosophy in Berlin, eventually receiving a doctor's degree in philosophy (from Jena). Marx then proceeded to become a writer, editing a left-wing political periodical in Prussia, but censorship issues there drove him first to Paris and several other cities, eventually landing him in London, where he would live out his life.

Marx is in many ways the *opposite* of Adam Smith. The Scotsman had argued that when every man pursues his own self-interests, "this would result in an outcome beneficial to all, whereas Marx argued that the pursuit of self-interest would lead to anarchy, crisis, and the dissolution of the property-based system itself." (See Sylvia Nasar, *Grand Pursuit*, for documentation on this material.) Smith had a generally positive outlook on the human condition if only governments would honor man's "natural liberty"; Marx believed all governments were corrupt and oppressive. Smith believed that the "invisible hand" would boost everyone along and raise all ships, while Marx believed that the "iron fist of competition" would pulverize workers, even while it enriched those who owned the means of production.

In 1848 Marx met Friedrich Engels in Paris and the two men wrote the pamphlet, *The Communist Manifesto*. Later, in London, he would pursue the work that he dreamed of writing, *Das Kapital*, or, in English, just *Capital*. Marx believed that in economics, being human involves an effort at changing the world around us by labor, and so, *labor* is crucial to what it means to be human. But older economic systems had robbed people of their ability to do that, especially the manorial system, which utilized other person's labor to bring wealth to the barons, the bishops, and a few others. *Capitalism* (this was Marx's term, which is why we use it here) was better in that it gave people some access to some goods and services needed for happiness, but capitalism is only *quantitatively* better that manorialism, not *qualitatively*. In the older system people had to turn over the produce of their farms to others, while in capitalism people have to sell their labor for wages. Those

who own the means of production, the *bourgeoisie*, employ workers to produce goods that are then sold for excess *profit*, profit that
the owners keep for themselves. Profits were *inherently* unjust, in
Marx's view, since the *owners* of the *means of production* did not
generate them themselves.

Marx's economic theory was *materialistic* and deterministic.
Marx had made a close study of the writings of Georg Hegel, a
Berlin scholar who believed that history moved along a predict-
able and inevitable trajectory, always moving toward a higher
consciousness (what Hegel called the *Geist*) and a more just and
advanced social and political culture. Marx borrowed from Hegel,
arguing that the Roman slavery system had collided with manorialism, thus producing capitalism, but that now capitalism was
headed for a conflict with the new Socialism, the outcome of which
would be a new and more just system of political economy, Communism. Communism, the vision of a classless society based on
the equal distribution of all economic goods, was the goal toward
which history was aimed, but it had to pass first through capitalism, then Socialism (what Marx saw as the developing conflict in
his day) before utopia could be realized.

What was this Socialism that Marx trumpeted? What must
be done now (in 1848 when he wrote the *Manifesto*) so that a better world will one day dawn? He and Engels called for a ten-point
program: (1) abolition of private property, (2) heavy progressive
or graduated income tax, (3) abolition of all right of inheritance,
(4) confiscation of property of emigrants, (5) centralization of
credit in the hands of the state, (6) centralization of the means of
communication and transport in the hands of the state, (7) extension of factories and instruments of production owned by the state
(along with reclamation of waste lands by the state), (8) equal ob-
ligation of all to work, (9) combination of agriculture with manufacturing industries and the gradual abolition of the distinction
between town and country, and (10) the free education of all

children in public schools. All of this was to be increasingly placed under the direction of an authoritative administrative state.

Marx also contended that capitalism was inherently *class* based and that these class barriers, like the ones from the Middle Ages, could not ultimately be breached. The proletariat (workers) would remain the proletariat while the bourgeoisie would remain entrenched in their protected perches, enjoying the privilege and luxury of generational profits. This was unreformable in Marx's view, and the intractableness of this fact would be the key to the eventual rise of Communism. *Class conflict* was one of the keys to future utopia, and focusing on such conflict in his writings was important to him in order to trumpet it to anyone who would hear him. Urging for class conflict to accelerate would be one of the keys to bringing about a just system.

Marx was not completely negative toward entrepreneurship. The free-market system, in Marx's view, has the ability to be a very powerful economic system because it is constantly improving the means of production. It can do this because of the advances in technology and because it has so much surplus value to work with. Marx expected, though, that a crisis would come upon capitalism when profits would eventually fall even as the economy was growing. One crisis would eventually become many separate crises, and the resulting trauma would in the end collapse the system when the proletariat, out of frustration, would eventually rise up and wrest the means of production from the hands of the bourgeoisie. "The worse things got," he reasoned, "the better the odds of revolution." Marx and Engels argued that this eventuality was "inevitable." "Workers of the world, unite!"

Marx believed that capitalism was unreformable. He witnessed with his own eyes the problems associated with the industrialization of England: long work hours for children, cramped and dangerous work conditions, dirty tenement housing for workers in the city, and short life spans for many urban workers. These are all things that Charles Dickens would also write about in his novels. Marx died in 1883, the second volume of his *Capital* still unfinished. Had he lived a few more years he would have watched the reforming of the free-market system, as workers were paid more, they worked fewer hours, and children and women and indeed everyone worked in cleaner and safer conditions. Some of this happened through legislation in England and also in America, but it would have happened even without legislation. Why? Because as industrialization moved forward the business owners began to discover that there was more than one kind of *market* in the free market. Marx and other critics focused exclusively on the consumer market in the system and concluded that this was all that business owners were concerned with. But before long it became clear that there were other markets, and one very key one: the market for *workers*. When Henry Ford began paying his assembly line workers five dollars a day, three times the average at the time, he sent a signal that was heard around the entrepreneurial world. There was a competition for consumers, but now there was also a competition for workers, and in the case of Ford's company, the workers were now also the consumers of their own product, because they could afford to be.

But then something happened. In October 1929 the stock market crashed, a crash that was followed by a prolonged recession known as the Great Depression (see earlier discussion in chap. 5). Marxists thought that this recession ratified what Marx had said all along. Entrepreneurialism is unsustainable and will eventually collapse under its own weight, in their view. But then World War II fired up and the free market was back in business under the influence of government spending. In the meantime (1936), a Cambridge economist named John Maynard Keynes (pronounced "canes") had written a very technical economic treatise called *The General Theory of Employment, Interest and Money*. In this book he argued that Marx had not been *completely* correct, that entrepreneurialism was reformable, but that it could not be left to itself for such reforms. Only governments could reform the free-market system.

Then came the book's most enduring claim: "Mass unemployment had a single cause, inadequate demand, and an easy solution, expansionary fiscal policy." To boil that down to its basics, Keynes was saying that when there is mass unemployment, the government must insert itself into the economy with significant stimulus spending. Of course, if there is mass unemployment, it is also likely that government spending resources will be at low ebb. So, in such situations, governments must either *borrow* heavily in order to stimulate the economy or they must *raise taxes* on the wealthiest persons in society or both. When they insert such a fiscal *stimulus*, unemployment will go down. This is Keynesian economics at its most basic level, what we might call the governmental management model. And many of the most prestigious and liberal (the two terms mean much the same thing in many halls of academia) economists in *America*, the country that is the prime example of what Smith's free-market theory could produce in our world, are Keynesians to the core. Not all of them, but most. And they also serve as advisors to kings, parliaments, and presidents.

The Great Recession: The Keynesian Test

I am writing these words in the summer of 2012. For the last four years (or a bit longer) we Americans have felt the sting of what some are now calling the Great Recession. Technically the recession is over, but unemployment has been over 8 percent for about forty months. Yet, early in his presidency, Barack Obama with his Keynesian economic advisors in tow initiated and passed in Congress a massive Keynesian "stimulus" package that totaled nearly $1 trillion. If Keynes was right, this "expansionary fiscal policy" ought to have done the trick and brought unemployment down. It did not. When the stimulus bill was passed, unemployment was around 7 percent. Over the next year and a half it soared to nearly 10 percent, then inched down to just over 8 percent, where it stayed for months. President Obama had promised in speeches that this stimulus would bring unemployment down to 5.6 percent by 2012. After all, did he not have smart advisors who were assured that Keynes was correct? Weren't these same advisors absolutely certain that Adam Smith was wrong, that the Great Depression had proven that, and that the day of free-market economics was past?

I have already introduced Georg Hegel, who taught philosophy in Berlin until his death in 1831. Marx and many other liberals and progressives were disciples of Hegel, as I have noted, and Hegel had taught that society is evolving, becoming more humane all the time. He believed that in the near future (remember he died in 1831) society would become so evolved and humane that we would be able to put our trust in the administrative state to create a better society for us. It would employ the most highly educated intellectuals in carrying out this great task of governance, and, being highly educated, they would be the most *just* and the wisest of administrators. After all, is not an advanced education the best pathway to becoming wise and just? When that time comes, Hegel had taught, governments must do everything they can to eliminate obstacles to such just administration, and all governmental leaders must walk in unity to do what they know needs to be done to create the very best society possible.

That was Hegel's dream, and it is a dream that we are living right now, though the dream seems a little unbelievable these days. Some dreams come true, but not all of them. The president got what he wanted in the stimulus; since both houses of Congress were led by Democrats, there was nothing the Republicans could do to stop it. And here we are. Did you ever have two different dreams the same night, and then sometime later it was as if the two had merged? We are seeing the merging of the Hegelian and the Keynesian dreams. We have added over $5 trillion to our national debt in four years, a million fewer Americans are working than four years ago, we have massive new entitlement programs, and things look a bit bleak, if not nightmarish.

We have seen this before, right here in our study. What we have witnessed in recent years in America, first under George W. Bush with his extension of subsidies to various industries and his expansion of the federal government, but far more dramatically with Barack Obama's massive overreach of Washington, is the modern manifestation of Solomon's and Rehoboam's attempt to create a great and magnificent administrative state. In our day, as in theirs, it is all being done ostensibly "for the good of the people." In reality, it is being done for the glory of politicians and as a pathway for them to seize ever more and more power. It is nothing new. Both Roosevelts, under the influence of Hegelian advisors, attempted the same thing. So did Woodrow Wilson, the original advocate of "don't let a crisis go to waste," when he injected the United States into World War I. Lyndon Johnson perfected this with his Great Society policies, believing that the federal government could solve all societal problems. Even Richard Nixon, who secretly admired Nietzsche, affixed price controls, raised tariffs, expanded the EPA, enforced Great Society legislation, and sought for (but did not achieve) a guaranteed minimum income for Americans not connected to work or achievement—all Keynesian ideas. Bill Clinton, though he balanced the federal budget (under duress from a majority Republican Party in Congress), enacted Keynesian policies throughout his presidency, as have the last two presidents, as we have seen.

It appears that we have abandoned our heritage! Only Calvin Coolidge and Ronald Reagan (and perhaps Dwight Eisenhower), of all US presidents in the last century, have attempted to craft policy that is consistent with the kind of political economy that made this nation the economic powerhouse and ideological bastion for freedom in the first three centuries (going back to colonial days) of its existence. Have we sold our birthright for a bowl of stew (Gen. 25:27–30)? Or have we made a Faustian bargain, selling our soul to the devil so we might have a semblance of peace and economic security, though at a price that is becoming increasingly higher every year? And it is not just the price in dollars that I am worried about. The bigger price is the loss of our souls, and the souls of our grandchildren. This is true for us both as Americans in general and as American Christians in particular. Israel was never the same after Solomon and Rehoboam. We may never be the same either.

Conclusion

Whew! If you read this entire chapter in one sitting, you must be a bit light-headed at this point! In this chapter we have sought to trace the history of political economy. We examined the relationship between political and economic systems in post-Roman Europe, the subtle influences brought on by the Crusades, and then the shifts that occurred in so many ways as a result of the discovery of the Western Hemisphere. We then examined the three major competing systems of economic theory that have arisen over the past 250 years, free market, Socialism, and the governmental management models. We finished by looking briefly at where America stands at these crossroads. In recent years we have been enduring the Great Recession under a presidential administration that sometimes sounds Keynesian and sometimes Marxian. The future is uncertain. But before we complete our survey it will be helpful to put this discussion of political economy back into the context of Christian theology and the influence of the church. And remember that we are looking at these issues through the lens of Baptist beliefs and practices. So just what is a "Baptist political economy"?

Study Questions

1. Do your best to give a definition of "political economy." Now try to explain how the definition differs between free market, Socialist, and governmental management approaches to political economy.

2. In the above discussion of mercantilism we pointed out that the wealth of nations in that way of understanding had to do with how much gold a nation had. How did Adam Smith critique that, and what do you think Marx believed constituted the wealth of nations?

3. Given the difficult economic conditions that are the rule in many European countries today, do you think that the way forward is just to go back to simple farming and living off the land? Back to the manorial way of life?

4. Explain why trade is the crucial element that enables economies to grow, using examples from the Crusades, the opening up of the Western Hemisphere, and the rise of industrialization.

5. Explain why, in mercantilism, trade *is* war. Explain why, from the free-market perspective, that notion is wrong.

6. How does the history of Israel and its political dissolution during and after Solomon's and Rehoboam's reign illustrate what is at stake in America today?

For Further Reading

Bethell, Tom. *The Noblest Triumph: Property and Prosperity through the Ages.* New York: Palgrave Macmillan, 1999.

Brown, Stephen R. *Merchant Kings: When Companies Ruled the World, 1600–1900.* New York: Thomas Dunne Books, 2010.

Diamond, Jared. *Guns, Germs, and Steel: The Fates of Human Societies.* New York: W. W. Norton, 2005.

Heather, Peter. *Empires and Barbarians: The Fall of Rome and the Birth of Europe.* New York: Oxford University Press, 2010.

Skousen, Mark. *The Making of Modern Economics: The Lives and Ideas of the Great Thinkers.* 2nd ed. Armonk, NY: M. E. Sharpe, 2009.

Soll, Jacob. *The Information Master: Jean-Baptiste Colbert's Secret State Intelligence System.* Ann Arbor: University of Michigan Press, 2009.

Stark, Rodney. *God's Battalions: The Case for the Crusades.* New York: HarperOne, 2010.

Sylvia, Nasar. *Grand Pursuit: The Story of Economic Genius.* New York: Simon & Schuster, 2011.

Baptists and Flourishing | 7

In the previous chapter we have seen that theories of political economy in the last two hundred years or so have produced three primary models: the free-market model (Smith), the Socialist model (Marx), and the governmental management model (Keynes). Which is most consistent with Christian principles? Christian authors and advocates can be found in all three camps. The free-market model was adopted by many Christian thinkers in the nineteenth century, but it also had its critics. The Marxist model has been adopted by, especially, liberation theology in its various manifestations. And in more recent times, theological liberals and liberal evangelicals have found much in the Keynesian model to commend. We will briefly lay out these issues and offer comment.

The Bible and Economics

We have to say that the Bible does not explicitly lay out a theory of economics in a political context. But it does address issues of freedom, the use of resources such as money and time, justice, generosity, and governance, as we have discussed in the previous chapters. The Bible is God's Word and is not only the authoritative rule or standard for all faith, doctrine, and practice in the church but also in all of life. The Ten Commandments summarized in the commands to love God supremely with all that we are and have and to love one's neighbors as oneself are moral obligations for every human being to fulfill by God's grace through the obedience of faith, which works and expresses itself by love. Thus Scripture on these and other matters reveals God's moral will, direction, and purpose for humanity in the broadest of terms imaginable, as broad and as deep as his kingdom and his righteousness. This is not to suggest that any of the three primary models of political economy being considered can serve as some kind of theocratic utopia. Rather, this caveat is included here for the benefit of Christians and skeptics alike so the basis for the evaluations offered for these models is clearly understood.

So here then are the evaluations. There is no warrant for Socialist understandings of political economy since Scripture advocates a limited state and since it teaches that remedial justice, that is, the care of the genuinely poor, is *primarily* a function of the church and generous individuals who give of their own initiative to help others. We have argued here that in the modern world there is some role for government to help those who are *truly* helpless, but the Socialist model calls for a generally equal redistribution of the nation's goods, in Marx's words, "from those according to their ability to those according to their need." Socialism means that the state would become confiscatory in the taking of resources from some people and allocating them to others. That cannot be defended from the Bible, even though some liberation theologians attempt to meld Marx together with the Sermon on the Mount (see Ronald Nash, ed., *Liberation Theology*, for more on this). As the New Testament scholar Oscar Cullmann has shown, the notion of an expansionist state with a high level of authority over the details of people's lives cannot be proven from the New Testament (*The State in the New Testament*). In chapter 4 of this book, dealing with government, I argued that Baptists, Free Church advocates, and Anabaptists have seen Scripture as teaching that governments must be limited, lest they take on the role of God over their subjects. Over time, as "state-church" models have diminished in the world, other Christians, such as Abraham Kuyper, a Dutch Reformed scholar and politician, have agreed. Government must serve the people, and because of that, it cannot be granted large powers.

If that is true, then the Keynesian model also fails the test. While this model does not call for a more or less equal distribution of resources to all persons, it does grant to government sweeping powers that have no biblical justification. Furthermore, if it is linked with the Hegelian perspective that intellectuals employed by the administrative state will be able to govern with justice and wisdom so that all are bettered by their governance, that is very problematic for evangelical Christians, Baptist or otherwise. Scripture teaches that all humans are sinners. A PhD from Harvard does not diminish that, and might even make it worse if those elites believe that their education makes them morally better people. Arguably the smartest group of people in the twentieth century were intellectuals living in Germany in the 1930s, and they used their great brilliance in the support of a mad dictator! The Bible does not teach that society is going to get better and more moral over time but that the only hope for salvation lies in the second advent of our Lord and Savior, Jesus Christ. That does not mean, of course, that Christian people should not be concerned about justice and generosity in this world. It does mean, however, that governments will not be able to usher in a utopian society in an age in which both the poor and the rich, both the governed and those who govern are prideful and covetous, since all alike will have the proclivity to seek their own at the expense of others. That "own" that they seek may be wealth, it may be political power, or it may be the satisfaction of a particular vision for society. There must be checks and balances on all.

That leaves us with Smith as an option—the free market. We have argued in this book that free markets are consistent with Scripture, but we need to add a further comment. Smith's model has been critiqued on the basis that it is essentially justified selfishness. It certainly does begin with the individual and his concerns about his own life. But it is not just *his* life, but the life of his *family*. It is perfectly scriptural for us to be concerned about the financial and physical well-being of our wife, husband, children, parents, and so on. The Bible itself teaches that (1 Thess. 4:10–12). Consider also the absence of such concern and how that overburdens a society's welfare system. And something about Smith that is often overlooked is that he spoke as much about *benevolence* as about the self, and that justice is just as important in economic transactions as any other consideration. And in free-market economics, unless fraud is perpetrated or extortion applied, *justice* will be part of the exchange. In free-market transactions, both buyer and seller benefit from every trade. "It is not from the benevolence of the butcher, the brewer, or the baker, that we expect our dinner, but from their regard to their own interest." I have my interest, and you have yours, and economic transactions only occur when both are benefitted.

Then there is another concern. Entrepreneurship is a good thing. To invent a new and better mousetrap or a new machine that makes life more manageable or a new way to market goods and services that helps people—these are all wonderful things to be able to do, and they help us carry out the Genesis 2 mandate—to subdue the earth and make it serve us, our families, and our communities. But as an economics scholar named Thomas DiLorenzo has pointed out, there are two types of entrepreneurs—market entrepreneurs, and political entrepreneurs. He says, "A pure *mar-*

ket entrepreneur, or capitalist, succeeds financially by selling a newer, better, or less expensive product on the free market without any government subsidies, direct or indirect." This type of entrepreneur is philosophically and pragmatically committed to the ideals laid out by Adam Smith. Such an entrepreneur attempts to please the consumer, whether through quality, quantity, or cost (or usually some combination of those) of that which is produced, whether goods or services. Pleasing the consumer means *sales* and *productivity*, and so, is the pathway to business success. "By contrast, a *political entrepreneur* succeeds primarily by influencing government to subsidize his business or industry, or to enact legislation or regulation that harms his competition." This type of "entrepreneur" accomplishes his goal, which is generally the same goal of the market entrepreneur—sales of goods and services—primarily by currying political favor, not by producing something of superior *quality*.

DiLorenzo gives the following illustration. If you are in the mousetrap industry, you can become successful by building *better mousetraps* than other manufacturers and so attract a customer base and convince consumers that you have a better and more economically viable product than your competitors. On the other hand, you might instead lobby Congress to prohibit the importation of (or charge a heavy tariff on) all foreign-made mousetraps. The first is *market* entrepreneurship and the second is *political*. The American economy has always included a combination of both types, "self-made men and women as well as political connivers and manipulators," and the late nineteenth century witnessed the increase of both types, *in spades*.

The reason it is important to distinguish philosophically and historically between the two kinds of market-based approaches is that is that *only* the market entrepreneur is an *authentic free-market advocate*. The political entrepreneur is a "neomercantilist," that is, he wishes, like merchants in the mercantilist systems of the

Middle Ages, to get something by finding favor with politicians. The reason is clear. The mercantilist economies, such as those of Charles II of England and Louis XIV of France—periods (1600s) in the history of those countries when kings saw themselves as given divine right by God to lord it over every aspect of their country's identity—were comprised of heavy government intrusion into the economy to satisfy king or merchants or both, but only those merchants or industries who, for whatever political reason, curried favor with the *Crown*.

We seem to be headed back in that same direction. The federal government picks out who it wants to support based on philosophical concerns (or, worse, cronyism) and sees to it that those industries (or companies) get subsidized federal support—support that comes from other people's money. Meanwhile, other industries are penalized by regulation and higher taxes and costs, which turn into bills to pay that are pushed down to consumers that then cause prices to be inflated, which creates more of a drag on other people's money. It ought not to be that way. Let people build businesses, and if they thrive, they thrive. If not, well, maybe there is a reason.

The "Baptist" Contribution

For me and those of us in the Free Church (baptist) tradition, this discussion is highlighted by the fact that our very existence (see chap. 4 on government) was threatened early on the Continent and even in England by heavy-handed governments that thought they knew what was the right thing to do in regard to people's religious lives. We do not believe the government knows what the answer ought to be for people's religion, nor does it know what to do in regard to picking and choosing winners and losers in the economy and then expecting the citizens to foot the bill through taxes and increased costs. But that does not mean that some Baptists have not sided with Marx and Keynes or with some similar theory of political economy.

In the nineteenth century several Baptists were part of the Social Gospel movement and others were moderately Socialist. Walter Rauschenbusch was the most visible spokesman for the Social Gospel movement until his death in 1918. Though he rejected Marxism, his critiques of the free market sounded ominously similar. Rauschenbusch combined a liberal theological education with a warm evangelical heart, and this is all reflected in his approach to "social justice." He had studied closely the work of the German liberal, Albrecht Ritschl, who believed that the kingdom of God was social and was grounded in history, and that both justification and reconciliation (biblical terms) would be accomplished by the transformation of society in this age. Rauschenbusch affirmed these ideas. Ministering near Hell's Kitchen in New York City, Rauschenbusch saw the task of the church as the redemption of the social order. His vision was of a City of God on earth in which the *enlightened* church with a *liberalized* theology would cooperate with an *enlarged* administrative state that would use its coercive powers to equalize the distribution of goods to all citizens so that *none* would be in want, and thus bring the *kingdom of God* to the modern world.

Later, Harry Emerson Fosdick sounded clearly Socialist chords (he also was not a thoroughgoing Marxist) in his rejection of the free market. He believed that the church should be the champion for *economic reform* in the nation, for *redistribution* of wealth, and for *empowering unions* to discipline big business. Far more theologically liberal than even Rauschenbusch, Fosdick preached a sermon during the Great Depression titled "The Ghost of a Chance" in which he laid out his views, denouncing economic injustice and blasting free-market economics. Some in Congress saw this sermon as a red flag and classified Fosdick with the "pink intellectuals and sobbing socialists." This New York preacher and theologian was convinced that the social implications of the gospel were far more significant than issues of personal salvation. He went much farther than the older Social Gospel in eviscerating the heart of orthodox, evangelical theology.

Late in the twentieth century several prominent Baptist evangelicals joined in the critique of the free market, most notably Ron Sider and Craig Blomberg. Both Blomberg and Sider hit hard at evangelicals living the "American Dream," and call on them to give away most of their income, believing that if all Americans tithed progressively larger amounts and if those tithes were used to support the poor, that the poor of the world could be fed by American Christianity. I have looked at "the math" on that and can tell you that they are wrong. They also call on the federal government to tax the rich at a much higher rate in order to provide relief, thus joining Rauschenbusch in his approach to economic redistribution and the enactment of a vision of social justice.

With these exceptions in mind (and there are more), most Baptists, especially Baptist evangelicals, have strongly contended for the free market. In the nineteenth century, Baptist intellectual Francis Wayland contended, in his book *Elements of Political Economy*, that America's commercial success was based on the model laid out by Adam Smith, that it had the potential for great blessing, and that it had to be accompanied by limitations on the expansion of the federal government. In true free-market fashion he declared, "The principles of supply and demand were seen as part of the divinely ordered structure of the world." In other words, for Wayland, the world that God has given us points to the truth of free-market economics. He further argued that being wealthy was not a sin in and of itself. "The right of property is founded on the will of God . . . as made known to us by natural conscience, by general consequences, and by revelation." The example he pointed to was Nicholas Brown, the patron of Brown University, a man who had combined a gift for making money with a commitment to Christian ideals of *benevolence*. Wayland further observed that Brown had done so not at the end of a life dedicated to making a fortune, like some who after "the love of wealth, eating like a canker into his soul, had paralyzed every generous sentiment" and who then give away a fortune as if to *atone* for their greed. No, Wayland said, Brown had done so all his life.

Wayland's approach was completely consistent with the theology of human dignity we have discussed already and seen in the life and work of Conrad Grebel, Menno Simons, and Roger Williams. Those men had little to say about the interface between economics and politics, but their views on government, religious liberty, freedom of speech, and voluntaryism in religion are perfectly compatible with a free-market approach. In the nineteenth century the religious landscape of America was changing. Whereas earlier the largest denominations were Congregationalist and Anglican (the Protestant Episcopal Church after the Revolution), throughout the nineteenth century these denominations declined. Some American church historians, such as W. W. Sweet, have concluded from this that American religious fervor declined after the Revolution. But nothing could be more wrong! Christianity flourished on the frontier, but not the older traditions. They were inherently bound to state-church models, models that just did not fit in Tennessee, Ohio, and Indiana. Further, they were entrenched in educational models that demanded the highest standards of liberal education for their ministers, education in the nineteenth century that was saturated with the writings of "infidels" and "liberals" such as David Hume, Voltaire, Matthew Tindal, and Friedrich Schleiermacher. Small wonder that their churches were dwindling under the influence of preachers whose sermons reflected those ideologies.

Liberal theology and established churches were two reasons that older denominations declined while younger ones flourished, but there was an even greater reason: ecclesiastical entrepreneurship! The Baptist (and the American Methodists) actually pursued the growth of the churches and the spread of the gospel in an entrepreneurial manner, especially in the South. Several factors led to this. One, Baptist churches in the South were autonomous bodies, which meant that they did not have to wait for denominational machinery, which can grind very slowly, to endorse or catch up with church growth. They just went out and started new churches. Two, many Baptist ministers were bi-vocational (the farmer-preacher we have already discussed), which meant that there were more ministers in the churches and that they had greater flexibility for relocating. Three, the Baptist seminaries in the South continued to serve their churches and did not become independent "divinity schools" as many older denominational schools and even Baptist seminaries in the North had done. This kept them more evangelical and tied in to ministerial training and not just the educating of scholars. (See Roger Finke and Rodney Stark, *The Churching of America, 1776–2005* for more on this.) In other words, as America's entrepreneurial engine was marching west and spreading its wings, Baptists were also marching west and spreading the gospel. Baptist ecclesiology and ministry practice in many ways mirrored the spirit that was making America great. As the nation flourished, so did the Baptists.

In the twentieth century some of the most important voices in Baptist life showed great affinity to the free market and limited government. Examples include Carl F. H. Henry and Wayne Grudem. Henry's many writings make clear his call for limited government, his advocacy of the free market, along with pointed critiques of the horrors of Socialism throughout the twentieth century, and the biblical call to generosity on the part of evangelicals. He was a founding board member of the Institute on Religion and Democracy, his son Paul serving in the US House of Representatives from Michigan. He also served on the board of World Vision and spent many years promoting its programs of relief for the world's poor through voluntary giving. Henry was also a vocal defender of orthodox theology and of the Bible's inerrancy. Wayne

Grudem has also defended limited government and the free market, especially in his textbook *Politics according to the Bible* and in his book *Business for the Glory of God*. In both of these books he presents hermeneutical principles that are consistent with Baptist interpretations of church and state and are accepted by many non-Baptist Christians as well.

That is not the only part of the story to tell. One of the most influential Baptist ministers of the twentieth century was Martin Luther King Jr. King was educated in the liberalizing (or neoorthodox) theology that was prominent in the 1940s, studying under stellar scholars such as Reinhold Niebuhr. Though Niebuhr was no conservative, his mature theology took full account of human sin and the need for redemption, both personal and societal. King appreciated the Social Gospel theology of Rauschenbusch, but at the end of the day, rejected it. He believed that the idea that government and churches could somehow come together to improve the lot of humans was an illusion, and he likewise held out no hope, as Fosdick had, that some coalition of church, labor unions, and Progressive politics could solve the racial problems in this country.

King believed that a new generation was dawning. For him, the answer to the problem of racism lay in personal salvation and in appealing to the Christian consciousness of a nation by displaying the injustice of racism. His hope was that a younger generation of Americans would do better than their fathers had. In his 1963 Birmingham campaign he stated, "The purpose of . . . direct action is to create a situation so crisis-packed that it will inevitably open the door to negotiation." King was no Socialist, nor was he an advocate of liberation theology, nor did he ask for special treatment for blacks. He just wanted blacks to have the same opportunities as whites. In keeping with his Baptist heritage, mere weeks before his assassination, King told a gathering of workers, "All labor has dignity." King's concern was that black people in America had been cut out of the "American Dream," and he wanted them to have as equal an opportunity as whites to the table of flourishing in this great country. He was not looking for handouts for blacks in America. His understanding of human sin was as profound as that found in Augustine or Calvin. King also rejected any kind of strategy of violent coercion. What anchored Martin Luther King more than anything else was not his liberal theological education, but his deep roots in Baptist piety and ecclesiology, and the spiritual conversion that he experienced one night when his home was attacked with his daughter inside. King's approach to justice was color-blind; unlike some of his successors today (Jeremiah Wright and Jesse Jackson), it was not a plea for the administrative state to come to the rescue. While some of us would find some fault in some of the positions he took, we applaud him as a man who stood for biblical principles and for the Baptist heritage in the courageous way that he fought racism and injustice. I, for one, was deeply moved when he was assassinated (I was thirteen) and see him as one of the heroes of the faith.

Christian Ministry and Economics

I am sure that many overworked and overburdened pastors reading this little book are asking the question, "What have I to do with economics? I don't understand it very well, anyway, and I just don't see the connection between all of that and my ministry." I would like to offer some brief comments on why pastors and seminaries need to have something to offer to this field of enquiry as well as to the people whom they seek to serve both inside and outside the church.

First, the Bible deals with economic issues, as I have tried to show in this volume. It addresses matters of stewardship of our world (Gen. 1–3; Gen. 9:1–7), of God's ownership of creation (Matt. 6:25–30; Col. 1:16–20), and of economic shalom (Lev. 25:1–55;

Acts 2:42–47; 2 Thess. 3:6–10), and other important issues given more detailed discussion in the earlier chapters.

Second, an understanding of economics and especially of political economy can help us understand what is going on in the world around us. The general election of 2012 is impossible to follow without some understanding of the implications of Obamacare and its impact on Medicare, the federal deficit, and the long-term effects of continued deficit spending. The posturing on the part of Republicans and Democrats sometimes seems like little more than rhetoric, but the one who understands what is really at stake can help lead people to a better understanding of their responsibility in the public square.

Third, an understanding of economics can help us pastor our people more effectively by pointing to the need for a more comprehensive model of Christian discipleship. Many people in our churches just don't grasp that wealth is produced through work, how that in itself is a blessing to others, and then what God calls them to do with their wealth, even if they have very little of it. Taking a money management course is important to becoming a mature steward, but what most need more than that is a framework for understanding how politics, economics, and citizenship responsibilities fit into a broader discipleship model of life stewardship. In other words, they need an introduction to biblical oikonomia ("the law of the house"). And this applies to pastors and seminary professors every bit as much as it does to members of the congregation. A good place to start is by imparting some understanding of supply and demand, of fruitfulness and pay, and of how investments work (just to give a small sampling), because this will help God's people to grasp better the role they play every day in the broad sweep of God's mission in the world.

Fourth, our people desperately need to understand what I have called here, a theology of work and economics. People go to their jobs, but often just see that as a necessary evil in their lives to satisfy their immediate needs. They need a bigger picture perspective on the fact that God made them, in part, to work, and that all legitimate work glorifies God and through its fruitfulness, in turn, is a blessing to countless others. Work is an aspect of image; human beings without a task or who are lazy are not reflecting the image of God in which they were created. Many Christians do not realize that work appears in the Bible in advance of the fall and is included in God's evaluation of everything he had made, that it was "very good." Thus work possesses moral value and worth that survives the fall and remains intact even after God curses the ground. However, moral evil in the world as a consequence of human sin and the fall can and often does interfere with work (for instance, job loss caused by others' sinful mismanagement of a company, or physical inability to work due to illness or injury). Though frustrated and made more tedious by sin, work can and should be a duty that is equally a delight, even in a fallen world. Even more so when we realize that when we work, we are tangibly representing aspects of who God is and what he is like by the work we perform as well as the way or manner in which we labor at our various tasks in life.

Fifth, we need to help people understand the theological implications of politics. All political positioning has theological implications, as we tried to show by examining Augustine, Thomas Aquinas, Calvin, and the Baptists. In my Baptist tradition the relationship between theology and politics sometimes is strained, but really every tradition has to deal with that strain in our world today. Still, people need to understand the fundamental dynamics at play.

The Acton Institute through its Christian's Library Press is publishing four volumes in this series on work, economics, and related issues in which this volume is featured: Baptist, Pentecostal, Reformed, and Wesleyan. I encourage the readers of this book to read all four and weigh the relative merits of each.

Conclusion

Baptists are among the latecomers to the ecclesiastical world. Whether one takes us back to those furtive figures baptizing one another in Zurich in 1525 or to the little band of English Separatists doing the same in Holland in 1609, we do not have the deep roots of Roman Catholicism or Eastern Orthodoxy. But we have brought some things to the table, and we are sort of proud of that (hopefully in the right way). Most of us have been committed to limited government, to religious liberty, and to the relative autonomy of local congregations (though most of us also form associations of some kind with like-minded churches). We have generally stood for the rights of people to make their own way in life and to flourish in broad and varied ways. John Rockefeller was a Baptist entrepreneur who did that, as was Nicholas Brown. Both men testified to powerful conversion experiences, both men opposed the interference of government in the workings of business, and both men gave generously all of their lives to charitable causes, both churchly and otherwise. Those principles have marked out the "Baptist Way" for over four hundred years.

Study Questions

1. What examples of Baptists in this chapter stand for limited government and low government interference in the economy? Which ones do not?

2. How does the Baptist conviction about religious liberty impact a belief in limited government?

3. In what ways have Baptists emphasized the importance of entrepreneurship?

4. Do you think one's view on the authority of Scripture has an impact on how one views government and its limited role?

For Further Reading

Bebbington, David W. *Baptists through the Centuries: A History of a Global People*. Waco: Baylor University Press, 2010.

Brand, Chad Owen, and David E. Hankins. *One Sacred Effort: The Cooperative Program of Southern Baptists*. Nashville: B&H, 2005.

Cullmann, Oscar. *The State in the New Testament*. New York: Scribner, 1956.

Finke, Roger and Rodney Stark. *The Churching of America, 1776–2005: Winners and Losers in Our Religious Economy*. Rev. ed. New Brunswick, NJ: Rutgers University Press, 2005.

Sowell, Thomas. *Basic Economics: A Citizen's Guide to the Economy*. Rev. ed. New York: Basic Books, 2004.

Epilogue

One of my friends says that whenever we have looked at an issue, especially a political or economic issue, we should stop at some point and ask, "And then what?" The "And then what?" before us now is certainly frightening. Looming debt, an increasingly avaricious welfare system, and city officials that would rather have adult book stores than Chick-fil-A restaurants because the head of that organization stands for traditional marriage values ought to make us realize how deep is our difficulty. We are facing a federal bureaucracy in the Obama administration that is encroaching on churches and their right to hold their values without government interference, in mandating that religiously affiliated organizations offer abortifacient and contraceptive insurance to their employees when that would entail a clear violation of conscience based on an organization's long professed religious beliefs. Without a change in our government, the "And then what?" question has some frightening answers. What has brought us here? Has it been our selfishness? Have we elected these people to office because they can get us another entitlement handout, another government contract, another financial bailout? The only final solution is the second advent of our Savior, the Lord Jesus Christ. But we do not know when that will be. In the meantime we must do what we can to slow the moral decay and restore sanity to our national situation. It is my prayer that God will give us abundant wisdom and grace to meet this challenge.

Bibliography

Augustine. *The City of God against the Pagans.* Edited and translated by R. W. Dyson. Cambridge: Cambridge University Press, 1998.

Bainton, Roland. *Here I Stand: A Life of Martin Luther.* Nashville: Abingdon, 1950.

Bebbington, David W. *Baptists through the Centuries: A History of a Global People.* Waco: Baylor University Press, 2010.

Beisner, E. Calvin. *Where Garden Meets Wilderness.* Grand Rapids: Eerdmans, 1997.

Bender, Harold S. *Conrad Grebel, c. 1498–1526: The Founder of the Swiss Brethren Sometimes Called Anabaptists.* Goshen, IN: Mennonite Historical Society, 1950. Reprint, Eugene, OR: Wipf and Stock, 1998.

Bethell, Tom. *The Noblest Triumph: Property and Prosperity through the Ages.* New York: Palgrave Macmillan, 1999.

Boles, John B. *The Great Revival, 1787–1805: The Origins of the Southern Evangelical Mind.* Lexington: University Press of Kentucky, 1972.

Brand, Chad, and Tom Pratt. *Seeking the City: Christian Faith and Political Economy; A Biblical, Theological, Historical Study.* Grand Rapids: Kregel, 2013.

Brand, Chad Owen, and David E. Hankins. *One Sacred Effort: The Cooperative Program of Southern Baptists.* Nashville: B&H, 2005.

Brown, Stephen R. *Merchant Kings: When Companies Ruled the World, 1600–1900.* New York: Thomas Dunne Books, 2010.

Cullmann, Oscar. *The State in the New Testament.* New York: Scribner, 1956.

Diamond, Jared. *Guns, Germs, and Steel: The Fates of Human Societies.* New York: W. W. Norton, 2005.

DiLorenzo, Thomas J. *How Capitalism Saved America: The Untold History of Our Country, from the Pilgrims to the Present.* New York: Three Rivers, 2005.

Engerman, Stanley L., and Robert H. Gallman. "The Emergence of a Market Economy before 1860." In *A Companion to 19th-Century America.* Edited by William L. Barney. Malden, MA: Blackwell, 2006.

Finke, Roger and Rodney Stark. *The Churching of America, 1776– 2005: Winners and Losers in Our Religious Economy.* Rev. ed. New Brunswick, NJ: Rutgers University Press, 2005.

Foster, Herbert D. "International Calvinism through Locke and the Revolution of 1688." In *The American Historical Review* 32, no. 3 (April 1927): 480–97.

Gordon, Bruce. *Calvin.* New Haven: Yale University Press, 2009.

Hall, David W., and Matthew D. Burton. *Calvin and Commerce: The Transforming Power of Calvinism in Market Economics.* Phillipsburg, NJ: P&R, 2009.

Harrison, Everett F., and Donald A. Hagner. *Romans.* Rev. ed. In Expositor's Bible Commentary 11. Edited by Tremper Longman III and David E. Garland. Grand Rapids: Zondervan, 2007.

Hatch, Nathan O. *The Sacred Cause of Liberty: Republican Thought and the Millennium in Revolutionary New England.* New Haven: Yale University Press, 1977.

Heather, Peter. *Empires and Barbarians: The Fall of Rome and the Birth of Europe.* New York: Oxford University Press, 2010.

Horner, Christopher C. *Red Hot Lies: How Global Warming Alarmists Use Threats, Fraud, and Deception to Keep You Misinformed.* Washington, DC: Regnery, 2008.

Johnson, Paul. *A History of the American People.* New York: HarperCollins, 1997.

Käsemann, Ernst. *New Testament Questions of Today.* Translated by W. J. Montague. London: SCM, 1974. Study edition reprint, 2012.

Kidd, Thomas. *God of Liberty: A Religious History of the American Revolution.* New York: Basic Books, 2010.

Kuyper, Abraham. "Sphere Sovereignty." In *Abraham Kuyper: A Centennial Reader*, ed. James D. Bratt. Grand Rapids: Eerdmans, 1998.

Lilla, Mark. *The Stillborn God: Religion, Politics, and the Modern West*. New York: Vintage Books, 2007.

Payton, James R., Jr. *Getting the Reformation Wrong: Correcting Some Misunderstandings*. Downers Grove, IL: InterVarsity, 2010.

Mueller, John. *Redeeming Economics: Discovering the Missing Element*. Wilmington, DE: ISI Books, 2010.

Olasky, Marvin. *The Tragedy of American Compassion*. Washington: Regnery Gateway, 1992. Distributed by National Book Network.

Rector, Robert. The Heritage Foundation. http://www.heritage.org/. See publications by the author.

Schmidt, Alvin J. *How Christianity Changed the World*. Grand Rapids: Zondervan, 2004.

Shlaes, Amity. *The Forgotten Man: A New History of the Great Depression*. New York: HarperCollins, 2007.

Sire, James W. *The Universe Next Door: A Basic Worldview Catalog*. 5th ed. Downers Grove, IL: InterVarsity, 2009.

Skousen, Mark. *The Making of Modern Economics: The Lives and Ideas of the Great Thinkers*. 2nd ed. Armonk, NY: M. E. Sharpe, 2009.

Soll, Jacob. *The Information Master: Jean-Baptiste Colbert's Secret State Intelligence System*. Ann Arbor: University of Michigan Press, 2009.

Sowell, Thomas. *Basic Economics: A Citizen's Guide to the Economy*. Rev. ed. New York: Basic Books, 2004.

———. "The Paul Ryan Choice." RealClearPolitics. August 14, 2012. http://www.realclearpolitics.com/articles/2012/08/14/the_paul_ryan_choice_115088.html.

Stark, Rodney. *God's Battalions: The Case for the Crusades*. New York: HarperOne, 2010.

———. *The Victory of Reason: How Christianity Led to Freedom, Capitalism, and Western Success*. New York: Random House, 2005.

Sylvia, Nasar. *Grand Pursuit: The Story of Economic Genius.* New York: Simon & Schuster, 2011.

Van Dam, Raymond. *Rome and Constantinople: Rewriting Roman History during Late Antiquity.* Waco, TX: Baylor University Press, 2010.

Wheatley, Alan B. *Patronage in Early Christianity: Its Use and Transformation from Jesus to Paul of Samosata.* Eugene, OR: Wipf and Stock / Pickwick Publications, 2011.

About the Author

Chad Brand (PhD, Southwestern Baptist Theological Seminary) is professor of Christian theology at The Southern Baptist Theological Seminary (Louisville, KY), where he has taught for thirteen years, and is associate dean of Boyce College. Previously he taught at North Greenville University. He has served as pastor of three Southern Baptist churches and interim pastor of several others. He is author or editor of fourteen books, including the *Holman Illustrated Bible Dictionary*. He and his wife, Tina, have three children and six grandchildren.